ENSLAVEMENT
in the
PURITAN VILLAGE

ENSLAVEMENT

in the

PURITAN VILLAGE

THE UNTOLD HISTORY OF
SUDBURY AND WAYLAND, MASSACHUSETTS

JANE H. SCIACCA

FOREWORD BY RACHAEL ROBINSON,
EXECUTIVE DIRECTOR OF THE SUDBURY HISTORICAL SOCIETY

THE
History
PRESS

Published by The History Press
Charleston, SC
www.historypress.com

First published 2025

Manufactured in the United States

ISBN 9781467157179

Library of Congress Control Number: 2024945302

Notice: The information in this book is true and complete to the best of our knowledge. It is offered without guarantee on the part of the author or The History Press. The author and The History Press disclaim all liability in connection with the use of this book.

To my husband, Tom

CONTENTS

FOREWORD

In the crisp month of January 2021, an email from Jane Sciacca found its way to my inbox, sparking a connection that would lead to a wonderful working relationship. Jane sought information about the Loring Parsonage for an upcoming presentation of hers in Wayland. Our communication was infrequent at first and then grew gradually to expand upon other topics. It was destined to be more than just a correspondence; it was the prelude to a journey through the annals of Sudbury's rich history.

Eventually, one fine day, Jane stepped through the doors of the Sudbury Historical Society, and our digital rapport transformed into a face-to-face meeting. Despite her residing in the neighboring town, the pandemic had kept us physically apart for an extended period. As Jane happily explained her research—spanning over two decades—it became evident that her dedication to the subject was nothing short of inspiring. She spoke about the individuals she had meticulously researched with a deep affection that breathed life into historical figures never known or recognized as part of the colonial history of Sudbury.

Jane's scope was not limited to Wayland; her research enveloped all of Sudbury, reaching even into the former areas that once bore the town's name. For those unfamiliar, Sudbury's original town center lay in what is now Wayland. It was established in 1638 and incorporated in 1639, and the first settlers made their homes on the east side of the Sudbury River. As families grew and the demand for land increased, the town spilled over to the

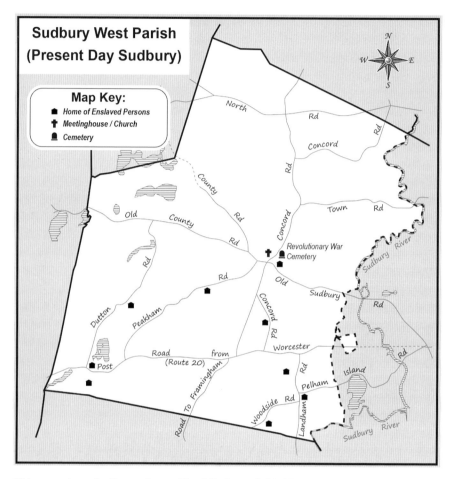

This page and opposite: East and west side of Sudbury divided into two parishes or precincts in the 1720s. The town employed two ministers, one on each side of the Sudbury River. The separation into two towns would not happen until 1780. *Map created by Brendan Decker.*

west bank of the river. A dispute arose when the west-side residents found it cumbersome to cross the river for church services each week. Litigious as Puritans often were, a court battle ensued, resulting in the construction of a meetinghouse on the west side in 1723.

This marked the beginning of Sudbury operating as two separate precincts. Post–Revolutionary War in 1780, the east side, reluctant to foot the bill for the war and cover the west side's share, formalized the separation. In this process, the east side relinquished the name Sudbury and its records, adopting the moniker East Sudbury for more than half a century until renaming itself Wayland.

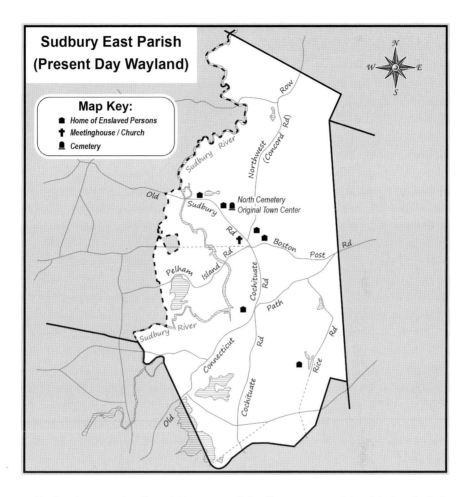

Reflecting on the first 141 years of Sudbury covered in this book, it is crucial to remember that these two towns were once united. Birth and death records simply list the town as Sudbury, irrespective of on which side of the river the event occurred. This fact, surprisingly unknown to many, often requires correction for genealogical researchers. In 1963, Sumner Chilton Powell penned *Puritan Village*, asserting Sudbury as a quintessential example of a perfect Puritan settlement. The title has endured, encapsulating Sudbury's essence through the years.

Despite the prevalent myth that the North was always free, the topic of slavery in Sudbury and the broader Northeast is frequently overlooked. Many New Englanders remain oblivious to the historical reality of slavery in the region. It is time to dispel the notion that the North was immune to this dark chapter of history. Jane, with unwavering diligence, has embarked on this crucial work. As you delve into the pages of this book, I invite you, the reader, to glean insights and knowledge, transcending the myths that have lingered for far too long.

—Rachael Robinson,
Executive Director of the Sudbury Historical Society

ACKNOWLEDGEMENTS

Turning my twenty-five years of research and a manuscript into an actual book required contributions from many wonderful old and new friends. First and foremost are three people whom I think of as my dream team. Fittingly, they represent both the east (Wayland) and west (Sudbury) sides of colonial Sudbury, and all are serious students of local history. Rachael Robinson is the executive director of the Sudbury Historical Society; Gretchen Schuler is the past president of the Wayland Historical Society and for many years chair of the Wayland Historic District Commission; and Douglas Currie is perfectly situated in Sudbury near the Wayland boundary to serve as a board member of the Sudbury Historical Society and on a planning committee at the Wayland Historical Society. Besides providing general guidance, they each have specific areas of expertise that greatly enhanced my work. Rachael was the graphics guru who prepared all graphics for submission and wrote the foreword. Gretchen is the author of most of the National Register inventories of historic buildings in Wayland and many in Sudbury as well. Her work on the maps created for this book made it possible to visualize the town in the days of slavery—a project well beyond my abilities to accomplish. Douglas, a serious historian of early New England and Indigenous peoples in particular, was familiar with a number of names that appear in this book as a result of his considerable research on colonial Sudbury. A museum professional, his interest in and careful study of the timeline found in the appendix inspired me to transform it from a research aid in writing the text to an integral part of the final production.

Two longtime friends and coworkers were also invaluable in readying the final manuscript: Charles Webster, retired National Park ranger, and Lois Davis, former curator of the Wayland Historical Society. Their knowledge and extensive reading of history made them the perfect people to individually apply a fine-toothed-comb approach to the manuscript as they checked the text, the index and the endnotes for accuracy and clarity.

Readers of the book at various stages of the writing offered comments that prompted me to make improvements. Special mention goes to Kevin Delaney, retired chair of the Wayland High School History Department, whose early reading of the text made me rethink the manuscript. Readers included Maria Cole, retired supervisory park ranger at Boston National Historical Park; and John Woodford, retired editor and journalist; as well as those mentioned previously.

This book is the product of over twenty years of research starting with microfilm readings of probate records at the Massachusetts Archives. The tradition of helpfulness of the staff extended into the age of the COVID pandemic. Special thanks to Caitlin Jones, reference archivist, who always answered my questions promptly, providing valuable information through links to scanned documents that unraveled so many mysteries. While I was willing to venture in person, because of her I was able to navigate the archives in the safety of my own home. The miracles of online resources never cease to amaze me. In the early 2000s, the Sudbury Archives was already online, a massive undertaking by the Town of Sudbury to make historical documents available to a wide audience. Their scope has only increased over time with additions from the Goodnow Library and the Archives of The Wayside Inn. Also crucial were the scanned documents I received from Nathaniel Smith, archivist of the town of Concord. I would not have been able to decipher the stories of several persons with ties to colonial Sudbury without his help. Laura Rankin, director of programs and education at the Framingham History Center, and Lauren Prescott, archives and online curator of The Wayside Inn Foundation, sent quality graphics that are used in this book. Graphic images are scarce when you are dealing with enslaved people over two hundred years ago, and their contributions are much appreciated. I am also grateful to Professors Jared Ross Hardesty, Richard J. Boles and Kenneth Minkema, who answered specific questions that I had after reading their books and watching their programs.

In-person visits to several repositories provided a welcome respite from the electronic world of the COVID pandemic. Laura Harms, local history librarian at the Goodnow Library in Sudbury, was particularly accommodating to my need to examine original documents, especially to supplement transcribed versions that were online. And it was nice to have someone who shared my interest and enthusiasm for the items I sought. Thanks to Sudbury town clerk Beth Klein and her staff, I was able to gather needed information in the town's vault. Thanks also to Rita Anderson and Jay Woodruff of Wayland's First Parish for allowing me to examine church records for the east side. Robert Leroux, director of assessing for the town of Wayland, and Kay Gardener-Westcott, curator of the Wayland Historical Society, who somehow also finds time to aid in town projects, granted me access to the assessor's records from the late eighteenth and early nineteenth centuries after Wayland became a separate town. I am of an age when handheld records are far more thrilling to me than electronic scans, so I appreciate the opportunities I was given to see and, dare I say, carefully handle the originals. Special thanks go to Sandy Coy for deciphering difficult-to-read ancient documents and to the legal acumen of Anette Lewis for translating legalese into English that I could understand.

Last, but never least, I would like to thank my family. Four family members took the time to read the manuscript and offer suggestions: my son Eric and young adult granddaughters Josie Brown and Lindsey Sciacca and my sister-in-law Linda Collins. For technical help that was far beyond my abilities, I could turn to my daughter Lisa Brown, a very patient college professor, and to my granddaughter Ashley Sciacca, a college student. Ashley turned my list of dates and events first into a spreadsheet and later into the timeline that appears in the appendix, while Lisa took time out of her busy schedule to help me organize and format my manuscript for publication. My husband, Tom, has been my most constant supporter, IT guy, proofreader and editor for the entire journey. I dedicate this book to him. I could not have done this without him.

INTRODUCTION

*While we bestow our earnest disapprobation on the system of slavery, let us not
flatter ourselves that we are in reality any better than our brethren in the South.
Thanks to our soil and climate, and the early exertions of the Quakers, the
form of slavery does not exist among us; but the very spirit of the hateful and
mischievous thing is here in all its strength.*
—Lydia Maria Child, 1833

In 1964, Sumner Chilton Powell won the Pulitzer Prize for *Puritan Village*, a history of the founding of colonial Sudbury in 1638, only eight years after the establishment of the Massachusetts Bay Colony. Today, colonial Sudbury encompasses two communities: Wayland (first called East Sudbury when the town divided in 1780 and later renamed Wayland in 1835) and modern-day Sudbury. Colonial Sudbury refers to both towns; the 1780 division appropriately signifies the waning days of enslavement in Massachusetts. Powell's premise was that "one town, well documented in relation to its specific origins, can serve as a representative study for most New England towns." His book follows Sudbury's first European settlers from the old world to the new as it became the second town settled west of Boston in the Massachusetts Bay Colony after Concord. The essence of the Puritan village remained largely intact throughout the seventeenth and eighteenth centuries as it evolved from a new venture to an established community. The dominant presence in the town remained white European settlers and their descendants. But there was another story that remained hidden and largely untold. While Sudbury's European origins and history have been comprehensively documented, existing histories of both modern Wayland and Sudbury make little or no mention of African Americans, many of whom were enslaved. Powell's book also fails to recognize an African American presence, and perhaps the period he covers predates their entrance to town. Alfred Sereno Hudson's 1889 *History of Sudbury, Massachusetts* devotes one page in his more-than-six-hundred-page book to "Servants," by which he meant African or African American slaves. Yet it turns out that the underside of the Puritan village is also well documented if one looks for it. There is no doubt that the task is infinitely easier and more satisfying with the digital resources of the twenty-first century than it was in the late nineteenth or even twentieth century. Over twenty years ago, when I began my research, it required in-person visits to libraries and archives and hours spent poring over microfilm. Now it largely consists of searching the internet for clues with less frequent visits on-site.

Sudbury's colonial inhabitants kept enslaved persons, bought and sold them, paid taxes on their human property and bequeathed them in wills. Both the enslaved population and their owners remained a very small proportion of the population, but the owners included some of the most prominent men in town. If you could afford an enslaved person and could use the help, there was no apparent stigma to owning one or two. Townsfolk were certainly aware that there were persons of color forced to live in their midst.

Our best source of information on the lives of enslaved persons comes from the *Journals of Rev. Israel Loring*, Sudbury's minister for sixty-six years from 1706 to 1772, covering most of the eighteenth century, when owning persons of color was legal and accepted in Massachusetts. More than any other records, his entries give a human face to the men and women he enslaved and those who were enslaved by others. His words bring to life those who occupied a netherworld between property and personhood in which glimpses of personalities emerge. Unfortunately, no words reveal the thoughts and perspectives of the enslaved persons on the events detailed in his journals.

The Sudbury Archives, an invaluable online resource of the town of Sudbury, provides easy access not only to Reverend Loring's journals but also to a number of references to enslaved people, including property deeds for the sale of slaves, census records, town meeting minutes and even an emancipation paper. These were available on the Sudbury Archives website in the early 2000s and have been expanded over time. They are an excellent starting point for records further afield.

One of the main obstacles to the study of enslaved persons in Sudbury, and New England in general, is that the Puritans, with few exceptions, referred to all those who served them, whether enslaved or free, Black, white, mixed-race or Indigenous, as "servants." One often has to become acquainted with the appropriate terminology for proof. A "negro man," for example left in a probate inventory with a value assigned signifies enslavement despite the omission of the word "slave," as do property deeds and emancipation papers. A full list of all sources appears in the bibliography and in the appendix.

Every attempt has been made to use only documented resources. In the few instances where I refer to reasonable conclusions without concrete proof, I will note it. And, as is the bane of all researchers, especially those who study the history of disenfranchised people, there are unfinished stories, dead ends or areas of confusion. These will be noted as well. As of this writing, there is no documentation of Indian enslavement in Sudbury, although it is quite possible that it existed in the early years of the settlement; therefore, all enslaved persons referred to in this narrative have African ancestry.

For many years I have studied and admired Wayland's nineteenth-century abolitionist Lydia Maria Child, who has been honored by induction into the National Women's Hall of Fame and the National Abolition Hall of Fame and is one of the few white faces in the National Museum of African American History and Culture in Washington, D.C. In 1833, Child published her groundbreaking work on slavery and prejudice, *An Appeal in Favor of That Class of Americans Called Africans*, in which she addressed the complicity of northerners, and from which the lead quote is taken. And although by 1833 Massachusetts claimed no enslaved persons or enslavers, Child did not have to look far into the past to uncover them right where she lived.

The following pages are an attempt to bring into focus the lives and experiences of Sudbury's enslaved persons and the slaveholders they served and to add to the research of enslavement in colonial Sudbury for others to build on.

PART I

THE SEVENTEENTH CENTURY

Chapter 1

THE BEGINNING AND END OF SLAVERY IN MASSACHUSETTS[1]

While the following dates and interpretations are subject to debate, it is generally accepted that the Massachusetts Constitution of 1780 (the year that Wayland and Sudbury became two separate towns) did not condone slavery. In 1783, that presumption was reinforced when court rulings were rendered in favor of several enslaved persons who had sued their masters for freedom. Since no separate law was passed in Massachusetts specifically banning slavery, it likely lingered into the 1780s and perhaps later. Nevertheless, in 1790, when the first federal census came out, Massachusetts was the only state that reported having no slaves. In Sudbury, the last documented reference to an enslaved person as of this writing occurred in a 1779 property deed for a "Negro garll" (girl) at the height of the American Revolution and three years after the Declaration of Independence proclaimed "that all men are created equal, that they are endowed by their Creator with certain unalienable Rights, that among these are Life, Liberty and the pursuit of Happiness."

As Massachusetts was the first state to abolish slavery, it was also the first colony to give legal sanction to it. In 1641, a document ironically called the Body of Liberties made it clear that Sudbury and all other towns in the Puritan colony had the freedom to enslave persons of color, whether Black, Indigenous or mixed race.

It is commonly known that when the Puritans founded the Massachusetts Bay Colony[2] in 1630, they brought with them white indentured servants bound to work for a specified length of time, usually seven years. As time

Artist's rendering of Mill Village, an early settlement on the west side of colonial Sudbury, by Alfred Sereno Hudson (1839–1907). *Courtesy of the Goodnow Library, Sudbury.*

went by the Puritans, in addition to importing white indentured servants, started using African and Native American men and women as well. With the Indian population of New England significantly decreased from the effects of foreign diseases even before settlement, Africans offered the potential for an abundant supply of laborers to address New England's chronic labor shortages. According to Professor Jared Ross Hardesty:

> *Although the local Indians made up the majority of the nonwhite labor force until around 1700, African slavery had many advantages. Unlike Native Americans, Black slaves were legally strangers in the fullest sense of the word. They had no claim to the land and were not familiar with the region's geography, making it harder for them to run away.*[3]

Undoubtedly, the greatest incentive to import Africans was the vital role the maritime trade played in the New England economy. Beginning in the seventeenth century and even more so in the eighteenth, New England, especially Boston, was the center of colonial shipping in America, which included the slave trade. Slave trading was a major source of the region's income. While most of the enslaved, and presumably the strongest, were sold to plantation owners in the South or the West Indies before the ships returned to their home ports, some enslaved persons were saved for the local market.

Governor John Winthrop, founder of the Massachusetts Bay Colony in 1630, recorded the importation of Black slaves from the West Indies as early as 1638, the year the Sudbury Plantation was founded. *Copy of a portrait of Massachusetts Bay Colony Governor John Winthrop donated to the American Antiquarian Society in the public domain.*

No less an authority than the founder of the Massachusetts Bay Colony, Governor John Winthrop, gives an account of the early slave trade in his journals from 1630 to 1649. The year 1638 is given as the probable date of the first importation of "Negroes" (the terminology used) from the West Indies into New England, and by 1644, Boston traders were importing enslaved persons directly from Africa. As Professor Ira Berlin explained in *Many Thousands Gone*:

> *Few slaves came directly from Africa…as there were more profitable markets in the south. Most slaves drifted into the northern colonies from the Caribbean Islands or the mainland South, an incidental remnant of the Atlantic trade. Since few northern traders specialized in selling slaves, slaves generally landed as special requisitions from merchants or farmers with connections to the sugar islands.*[4]

While slavery was accepted throughout the New England colonies, the concept of race did not take rigid form until the end of the seventeenth century. There was no legal restriction on intermarriage between whites and Blacks, for example, until 1705, when "An Act for the Better Preventing of a Spurious and Mixt Issue [*sic*]" became law in Massachusetts. Nevertheless, "Negro" servants gradually became equated with servitude without limits. To transform the concept of servants into "Servants for Life" (a euphemism for the enslaved that the Puritans preferred), in 1670, the General Court (legislature of the Massachusetts Bay Colony) amended the Body of Liberties so that the children of enslaved women were born enslaved. Not only did servitude without limits exist, but it was now hereditary.

Relatively little is known about enslaved persons who lived in Massachusetts before the eighteenth century, and population estimates vary. According to Professor Lorenzo J. Greene in *The Negro in Colonial New England*, fewer than one thousand Black people, free and enslaved, lived in New England in 1700 out of a total population of ninety thousand.[5] In addition to a small population, poor recordkeeping and a lack of recorded wills and newspapers accounted for a scarcity of information. Many of Sudbury's settlers, along with the rest of New England's colonists, were simply too busy clearing fields and raising livestock, dividing land and preparing for Indian attacks to have the leisure time to write letters or journals, if indeed they could write.

Were the owners of enslaved persons looked down on or shunned by society? Massachusetts native John Adams, the only one of the first five presidents of the United States who was not a slaveowner, wrote in 1819:

I have through my whole life, held the practice of slavery in such abhorrence, that I have never owned a Negro or any other slave, though I have lived for many years in times when the practice was not disgraceful; when the best men in my vicinity thought it not inconsistent with their character, and when it has cost me thousands of dollars for the labor and subsistence of free men, which I might have saved from the purchase of Negroes at times when they were very cheap.[6]

In fact, some of the most respected men in Sudbury, as was true throughout colonial Massachusetts and New England, were slaveowners. These included ministers, doctors, innkeepers, active members of the church and men who had served in the military with distinction. Among the very small number of men who held degrees from Harvard, both the Reverend Samuel Parris and William Baldwin owned enslaved persons.

Chapter 2

ENSLAVEMENT IN SUDBURY

The Early Years

While we do not know the exact date when enslaved persons first arrived in colonial Sudbury, those held in bondage may have been part of Sudbury households as early as 1654, only sixteen years after the town's founding. There was a difference of opinion at Town Meeting as to how a new land grant should be divided. Most of the freemen of the town wanted the land to be divided equally, but a minority had a different suggestion: "The lands shall be divided by the inhabitants according to their several estates and families and counting the family to be the husband, wife, children and such servants as men have that they have either bought or brought up."[7]

Why should this method of dividing land be proposed if no one had been bought or brought up, which certainly suggests the presence of enslaved persons? In any case, it would not take long to document an actual enslaved person in town.

THE CASE OF BENJAMIN CRANE AND HIS "NEGRO BOY"

Nineteenth-century abolitionist and author Lydia Maria Child[8] wrote, "Let us not flatter ourselves that we are in reality any better than our brethren in the South." Therefore, it is perhaps fitting that the first documentation of an enslaved person in colonial Sudbury is a record of unspeakable horror.

Alfred Sereno Hudson's painting of the Cakebread Mill on Wayland's Mill Pond depicts the first mill in colonial Sudbury. *Courtesy of the Goodnow Library, Sudbury.*

It serves as a poignant reminder that all enslaved persons were subject to the will and whim of a master regardless of the circumstances. Some were luckier than others, at least in regard to physical torment.

In *Sex in Middlesex*, author Roger Thompson combed the Middlesex County Court Records from the 1700s to discover this despicable act of Benjamin Crane of Sudbury toward his "Negro boy" in 1665–66. At the trial: "Witnesses described the boy wearing a 'geer of wire,' presumably a kind of muzzle, and a chain hobbling his feet. He had been heard screaming, 'O Lord! O Lord!' from a distance of a quarter of a mile off and he had many stripe wounds, some raw, some healed or partly healed."[9]

Contrary to what a modern reader might expect, the complaint was not brought by the "Negro boy" or those who witnessed his tattered back but by Benjamin Crane, who had suffered from multiple attempts by his young slave to run away. At the trial, the constable, who had witnessed the scars left by Crane's cruelty, testified that he had reproved the boy for "his untoward carriage to his master" and returned the boy to Crane, as the law required. As the constable retreated, he heard the boy's screams from his next beating. Other witnesses also testified to the repeated beatings that the enslaved boy suffered from Crane, but these comments were offered to demonstrate the boy's bad character and not the despicable acts of a brutal master.

Crane, born in Dedham, Massachusetts, had lived in a number of towns in both Massachusetts and New York before acquiring property in Sudbury circa 1664, shortly before the court case. He remained a citizen of Sudbury for the next twenty years and even appeared on a list of petitioners to the General Court in 1676 to be allowed to patrol the area in the wake of King Philip's War, which had recently reached Sudbury. Perhaps an article at Town Meeting on October 5, 1683, finally prompted him to move to the newly incorporated town of Stow, Massachusetts, where he spent the rest of his life. While Crane does not appear to have changed much as he aged, perhaps the townspeople had grown less tolerant of his behavior. The 1683 Town Meeting article stated:

> *It is ordered that Capt. Goodnow, & Tho. Read, Senr. forthwith at their best discretion make strict enquiry into the condition & usage of Benja. Crane's servant boy & make return therof* [sic] *to the Town; And that they also enquire in to the state & condition of sd Crane's daughter, suspected to be with child & hath no husband & to admonish her Parents carefully to inspect & look at her least* [sic] *worse befall her & them.*[10]

Who was this boy, undoubtedly Black and enslaved? Could he possibly be the same "Negro boy" who was so mistreated almost twenty years previously, or was he a new victim of this cruel master? So far, the question is unresolved, as no positive identifications can be made and the final judgment in the court case is as yet unknown.

Again, the story of Benjamin Crane and his enslaved boy(s) serves as a chilling example of Child's warning of the cruelty of enslavement inherent in the institution, no matter where it was practiced. No tests for the fitness to be a slaveowner were ever administered, no more than one's fitness to be enslaved.

THE NOYES FAMILY

In 1904, a genealogy of the Noyes family of Sudbury found it noteworthy that Colonel John Noyes (also known as John Noyes, Esquire), who died in 1785, "had much real estate and a considerable number of slaves."[11] Colonel Noyes was one of the most distinguished men in colonial Sudbury and, after 1780, in East Sudbury. His gravestone in Wayland's North Cemetery proclaims that he was "a Colonel of Militia in commission of the peace.

Home of Colonel John Noyes, "a man of considerable property, owning a number of slaves," including Cuff, Hagar and Cato. *Courtesy of the Wayland Historical Society.*

A member of the honorable legislature. A professor of the religion of the Gospel....For twenty-one years he was chosen to represent the town in the General Court."

The Noyes family involvement in slavery can be traced back to seventeenth-century Sudbury. Colonel Noyes's paternal grandfather, Joseph Noyes, was a native of Newbury in the Massachusetts Bay Colony who moved to Sudbury in the second half of the seventeenth century. *The New England Historical & Genealogical Register and Antiquarian Journal* reported the death of Elizabeth, a "negro" who belonged to him, in February 1675. Joseph Noyes was a person of distinction. He preceded his grandson in service to the town, serving as selectman for twenty-eight years, as well as constable and justice of the peace. And he, too, in the 1904 Noyes genealogy was touted as "a man of considerable property, owning a number of slaves,"[12] although none but Elizabeth has yet been identified by name.

Another Joseph Noyes predated the arrival of his kinsman in town. Born in England, he accompanied his father, Peter Noyes, a founder of the Sudbury Plantation, to the New World. This Joseph became a merchant in Charlestown and died in Barbados in the West Indies in 1661. In his will, he left his land there to his brothers and sisters, as he was a widower with no children. While no enslaved persons were mentioned in his will, Barbados was a center for the slave trade with numerous plantations using slave labor, and many landowners had ties to both. As both a merchant and a landowner, there is a strong possibility that Joseph Noyes owned and trafficked in enslaved persons.

Thomas Walker and Sambo

Thomas Walker[13] was a Sudbury transplant who moved in the 1660s from Boston to take charge of a free school. Soon after his arrival, he was listed as an innkeeper, but apparently he also remained a teacher. Perhaps he needed the two occupations, as four selectmen warned him in 1684 that he might have to relinquish his tavern sign due to possible excesses of intemperance occurring there.[14] In his 1697 will, Thomas left Sambo to his wife, Mary. In 1705, Mary married her second husband, Captain John Goodenow. By a document recorded in Massachusetts Land Records on June 16, 1719, Mary gave "negro Sambo" his freedom upon her decease, which occurred

The Thomas Walker House, also home to his enslaved boy Sambo, is believed to be the oldest dwelling still standing in Sudbury. *Photo from the Massachusetts Cultural Resource Information System.*

on November 4, 1731. While there is a record of Mary Goodenow's death, Sambo's death, whether he predeceased her or lived to experience his belated freedom, is thus far unknown.

A Boy Named Sampson

Several instances of enslavement at the dawn of the eighteenth century have tentacles that reach back to the waning years of the seventeenth. None is more evocative than the complex relations between Peter Goulding and his son-in-law, William Jennison, and "a negro sarvant [*sic*] boy" named Sampson. When Goulding died in Sudbury in 1703, he left his estate, including eight-year-old Sampson, to be administered by his wife, Sarah, who was named executrix of his will.

Goulding was born in England and probably arrived in the Massachusetts Bay Colony before 1665. He was reportedly a saddler by trade but seems to have also acted as an attorney at law. In 1670, Goulding aided a Bostonian, Joseph Deakin, in a lawsuit to recover a "Negro slave" named Katharina whom Deakin had sold in Virginia three years earlier. Goulding has been reported as present in Virginia at the time of the sale and likely to have been involved in it. Goulding's main interest, however, seemed to center not on the courtroom but in real estate. He acquired land in several places in the Worcester area. His arrival in Sudbury is dated circa 1694. He was said to have considered himself "a sojourner in Sudbury"[15] hoping to move back to the Worcester area when the opportunity arose. While Goulding did not live to return to Worcester, his family members did and have a long history there.

As reported by Harriette Merrifield Forbes in her history of Westborough, Massachusetts, Goulding, while residing in Sudbury, purchased land in Westborough for which he paid "one negro wench called Nanny, delivered at £25.10, and £10 in money."[16] The question arises as to the likelihood that Nanny was Sampson's mother. If so, she was sold away from Sampson when he was a very young child. The study of enslaved children in colonial New England has turned up multiple instances of children sold without a mother or a mother sold and separated from her child. We only have to go back to Benjamin Crane's "Negro boy" or Thomas Walker's Sambo to see other such examples in Sudbury. And in the case of Peter Goulding, as was true for Thomas Walker, only one enslaved person was listed in the inventory of his will, indicating the absence of any possible mother.

While it might seem that young Sampson had experienced enough trauma to last a lifetime after Goulding died, this was not the case once William Jennison and his wife, Elizabeth, entered the picture. Elizabeth was Peter Goulding's daughter and certainly not his favorite. In his will, Goulding leaves no room for misinterpretation: "To Elizabeth, the wife of William Jennison of Sudbury, I give 1s. [one shilling] or the value thereof, and no more, she having had higher keeping than the rest, and much out of my little [?] at her marriage; and I believe and partly know from her own mouth she has sought the ruin of me and my poor family in this life." Needless to say, Elizabeth and William did not inherit Sampson, yet on December 25, 1704, William Jennison sold Sampson to Thomas Browne of Sudbury for £30, claiming he had clear title to the boy. How could this be? Mysteriously, the death of Peter Goulding's wife, Sarah, is listed on various online sites as occurring on the same day as her husband's, and there is no record of her living past his death in 1703. Her untimely death becomes more plausible in the court records of the Jennison-Brown(e) trials. The court cases, which started in 1705 and concluded in 1708, were no longer about Sampson but about breach of contract.[17] Should Browne be reimbursed or not, given that Jennison actually had no right to sell Sampson? Did Sampson spend any time with Browne? And who should pay the considerable court costs as one party sued and countersued the other for three years? It turns out that Peter Goulding was in debt when he died, and two men had claims against his estate. Samuel Gookin, the sheriff, as was his legal right, took possession of Sampson, sold him and gave the proceeds to the claimants. Neither of the men lived in Sudbury, and the fate of young Sampson remains unknown.

William Jennison's fate is not a mystery. He held every prominent position in Sudbury before his next lawsuit over a matter of trespass in the early 1720s, which led to his loss of status. He then fulfilled his father-in-law's dream of moving to Worcester and becoming one of its most prominent and well-respected citizens. After his in-depth experience with the courts as a Sudbury resident, Jennison donated the land on which the first courthouse in Worcester was built in 1732 and served as a judge.[18]

A Woman Called Frank

When Thomas Read,[19] a prominent citizen living in the Landham district of Sudbury, died in 1701, he left a "Negro" woman named Frank to his "beloved wife," Arabella. This was a common occurrence in probate records. However, Arabella Read's will, which is dated 1716,[20] is remarkable for several reasons, not the least of which was the fact that she left a will at all, as it was more common for men to do so. Equally amazing was the stipulation that "'Frank' my Negro Maid Servant who was at my disposal," was not only given her freedom at Arabella's death but was also to receive all of her movable estate. Even more extraordinarily, Frank was also named executrix of Arabella's will. Perhaps this is evidence that Arabella's attitude toward enslavement changed during the years in which she owned Frank and lived with her. Whether Frank inherited anything remains unknown, as do her whereabouts in the subsequent years as a free woman of color. Evidence remains that, by the end of her life, Frank was not a woman of means. In 1742, Town Meeting appropriated money to pay Isaac Read for "Nursing of and Provision of Frank Negro in the year 1740," and the same Town Meeting also voted to compensate Dr. Ebenezer Roby for her medical care.[21] If Frank was in possession of any goods of value, she could have paid for her own treatments. It is likely that any money she inherited from Arabella Read went to the town for her support. According to Professor Greene in *The Negro in Colonial New England*, a law passed in 1703 required emancipators in Massachusetts to post a fifty-pound surety bond in case those freed from enslavement by their owners became a charge to the town. While we cannot be certain that the two "Franks" are the same person, it is reasonable to assume that they are. By the 1740s, Frank could indeed have been in need of care, as she was referred to as a "woman" when Thomas Read died in 1701.

Reverend Samuel Parris and Violet

Another early slaveholder in Sudbury was the Reverend Samuel Parris, who died in 1720. By the time Reverend Parris arrived in Sudbury, he had already secured his place in history for his connection to the Salem Witch Trials of 1692. In fact, the witchcraft hysteria started in his home in Salem Village while Reverend Parris was serving as minister. Reverend Parris's daughter Betty and her cousin Abigail Williams were reportedly mesmerized by his enslaved woman, Tituba. She told them disturbing stories of witches and magic learned in Barbados, where she had lived until Parris acquired her and brought her to Massachusetts with him. The Parris family were substantial landowners in Barbados, and young Samuel had been introduced to slavery there at a young age.

Above: The Noyes-Parris House, Wayland's oldest dwelling, was home to Reverend Samuel Parris and his enslaved woman, Violet. *Courtesy of the Wayland Historical Society.*

Opposite: Reverend Samuel Parris (1653–1720), Puritan minister in Salem Village during the Salem Witch Trials, later moved to colonial Sudbury and served as a schoolmaster.

In 1712, the widowed Reverend Parris moved to Sudbury with his second wife, Dorothy Noyes, a native of Sudbury and daughter of founding father Peter Noyes.[22] He served for a time as the town's schoolmaster and also pursued one of his former occupations as a merchant. At his death, he left an Indian girl named "Violate," as he spelled it, worth thirty pounds, to his son Samuel, along with some books, a silver seal, an agate case of knives, a horse and a colt. By "Indian girl," it is likely that Parris meant West Indian rather than Native American. This was how he always referred to Tituba, whose roots are still disputed but may have included African ancestry, as was the case for most enslaved persons imported from the West Indies. Equally as mired in mystery is the use of the word "girl" to describe Violet. What did that mean? Few enslaved people have recorded birth dates, which makes it impossible to know their ages. Was she a child, a teenager, a young woman or a grown woman who was referred to in this manner? Could she have been Tituba's daughter? Tituba was not a part of Reverend Parris's household at his death, and her relationship to Violet has been the subject of much speculation but not conclusively proven as of this writing. Today, Violet's dwelling place, the Noyes-Parris House, Wayland's oldest extant dwelling, stands as a reminder of how a major historical event can impact even a distant village.

PART II

THE EIGHTEENTH CENTURY

Chapter 3

THE HOMELIFE OF SUDBURY'S
ENSLAVED PERSONS[23]

ew people can imagine that New Englanders treated the enslaved like those on a southern plantation, and this was true to some extent. As Lorenzo Greene pointed out in *The Negro in Colonial New England*, "To meet the demands of New England's diversified economy, the slave had to be more skilled and more versatile than the average plantation Negro accustomed to the routine cultivation of a single crop."[24]

According to Professor Jared Ross Hardesty in *Black Lives, Native Lands, White Worlds*, "The way New Englanders deployed slave labor was unique. They largely attempted to adapt slavery to their traditional labor practices centered around the households and household production."[25] This was certainly the case in Puritan Sudbury.

Most households, of those who actually owned others, in Sudbury had only one or two enslaved persons in them, although David Baldwin, to give one example, left six upon his death in 1770. Enslaved males, most commonly referred to as the owner's "Negro man," typically worked on the farm alongside family members and occasional hired hands. An enslaved woman was referred to as a "maid servant" and worked primarily on household chores and childcare. As was true throughout New England, census data for Sudbury indicates that enslaved men tended to outnumber women, although with such small numbers the difference was not significant.

Unlike in the South, enslaved persons in Sudbury most often slept in their masters' houses and were considered part of the family. It was not unusual for those who were enslaved to eat with the people they served. For example,

Sudbury's Reverend Israel Loring recorded that Simeon, his enslaved boy, "was born in his house and brought up in his family."

The enslaved and their masters, who lived in close quarters, often shared the same diseases. Winters in particular brought households closer together when outside chores diminished. In 1729, during what Reverend Loring referred to as "a very sickly dying time with us at present," Dinah, enslaved by Hopestill Brown, died one day after her master. In December 1739, Reverend Loring recorded that his daughters, Elizabeth and Sarah, along with his maidservant, Hannah (later identified as Black), were recovering from the measles. Medical expenses were frequently incurred in many households covering both white and Black occupants.

While detailed accounts of the homelife and personal history of the enslaved are rare, we can get glimpses of them in two prominent families: those of Reverend Israel Loring, whose parsonage is now home to the Sudbury History Center, and the innkeeper Ezekiel Howe, proprietor of what is currently known as Longfellow's Wayside Inn.

Simeon and the Reverend Israel Loring

Many ministers in colonial New England owned enslaved persons. As the practice was condoned by the Bible, there was no stigma attached to slavery. In fact, Puritan ministers who had pledged their lives to serving God often felt that they were duty bound to instruct their "servants" to serve not only their owners but also their "Master in Heaven."

The Reverend Cotton Mather, arguably the leading light of Puritan clergymen, made this clear in *The Negro Christianized: An Essay to Excite and Assist the Good Work, the Instruction of Negro-Servants in Christianity* in 1706, the year that Reverend Loring came to Sudbury.

It is come to pass by the Providence of God, without which there comes nothing to pass, that Poor Negroes are cast under your Government and Protection. You take them into your Families; you look on them as part of your Possessions; and you Expect from their Service, a Support, and perhaps an Increase, of your other Possessions....Who can tell but that this Poor Creature may belong to the Election of God! Who can tell, but that God may have sent this Poor Creature into my Hands, that so One of the Elect may by my means be Called; & by my Instruction be made Wise unto Salvation!

The Loring Parsonage was home to the Reverend Israel Loring (1682–1772) and at least two enslaved persons, Simeon and his mother, Hannah. Today, it serves as the Sudbury History Center and Museum. *Courtesy of the Sudbury Historical Society.*

With this opportunity to Christianize an enslaved person came responsibilities befitting a man of the cloth to care for the weak and needy. According to Reverend Mather:

> *Masters, give unto your Servants, that which is Just & Equal, knowing that ye also have a Master in Heaven. Of what Servants is this Injunction to be understood? Verily, of Slaves.….As it is Just & Equal, that your Servants be not Over-wrought, and that while they Work for you, you should Feed them, and Cloath* [sic] *them, and afford convenient Rest unto them, and make their Lives comfortable; So it is Just and Equal, that you should Acquaint them, as far as you can, with the way to Salvation by JESUS CHRIST. You deny your Master in Heaven, if you do nothing to bring your Servants unto the Knowledge and Service of that glorious Master.*

And following Reverend Mather's instructions almost to the letter, Reverend Loring's treatment of Simeon, as captured in his *Journals*, is overflowing with caring and outright affection.

An entry in Reverend Loring's *Journal* referring to Simeon at the age of nine serves as one illustration. February. 3, 1743: "Sim Narrowly escaped of having both his Legs broken by a Log falling upon a Stone before the Schoolhouse Door. A Mercy Which I Wou'd take a due notice of and Return God thanks for."

The Reverend Cotton Mather (1663–1728) was an influential American Puritan clergyman who wrote *The Negro Christianized*, highlighting the Church's attitudes and treatment of enslaved Blacks. *Artist Peter Pelham.*

Even in the latter part of the nineteenth century, Alfred Sereno Hudson in his *History of Sudbury* extols Reverend Loring for his care of Simeon without any critique of the institution.

As previously noted, Simeon, as Reverend Loring divulges at the time of Simeon's death at the age of twenty-one in 1755, was born in "his house and brought up in his family." Unfortunately, none of Reverend Loring's journals containing the likely year of Simeon's birth in 1734 have yet been uncovered.

The comment "brought up in his family" has been the source of much speculation. While we do not find out the name of Simeon's mother until after his death, we never learn the name of Simeon's father. The only information we can deduce is where Simeon was born. Many ministers, along with the larger population of slaveowners, acquired their enslaved persons through inheritance, purchase or other means of exchange, but Simeon was born in Reverend Loring's household to a mother who was already enslaved there. Certainly Reverend Loring was carrying out the teachings of a devout Christian minister, but was there a more personal connection to these feelings? Did Puritan belief and individual circumstance intersect in Reverend Loring's actions? This still remains a mystery. Simeon, of course, did not have to be brought up in the Loring family. Reverend Loring as his owner had the right to sell him at any time. As we have already seen, Simeon would not have been the first child separated from his mother or have his mother separated from him. Simeon remained in the Loring household, with his mother present, throughout his life and was not emancipated until shortly before his death.

At the age of twenty-one, for unstated reasons, Simeon was given his freedom or, as Reverend Loring put it, "freed for my service and for himself." Simeon's "freedom" was short-lived. Less than a month later, on April 30, 1755, he was taken ill with colic but soon recovered. On May 10, Simeon became ill again and died. Reverend Loring noted in his *Journal*, "He was greatly beloved by the family and his death has drowned us in tears." A few days later, Reverend Loring wrote, "In the evening we committed the remains of Simeon to the dark and silent grave. A great number of the Congregation attended the funeral." On May 13, Reverend Loring added, "My wife before Simeon died took to her bed being overcome and worn out through labor of body and distress of mind about Simeon."

There is more to the story of Simeon that is not in Hudson's *History of Sudbury*. Reverend Loring also wrote on the day Simeon died, "The Lord sanctify this death to us all particularly to the mother of the deceased." Who was his mother? No earlier existing entry had ever even mentioned that Simeon had a mother, let alone one who remained in the Loring household. We find out the following week when Reverend Loring wrote, "Died Susanna(h) Harry sister to our hired woman servant Hannah....The loss of her son and now her sister." This tells us for the first time that Hannah is Simeon's mother.

We also find out from this sentence that Hannah was free (hence the "hired") by 1755. Hannah had not always been free, however. Earlier references in Loring's *Journals* call her "his Negro maid servant," a seemingly subtle distinction indicating that she was enslaved. There is no mention of when Hannah was given her freedom, but there is a plausible reason why she could have gained it. In February 1742, Reverend Loring recorded that his study caught fire, and "through the great goodness of God and endeavors of my servant maid Hannah and Mrs. Haiden it was extinguished and the house preserved."

What does this all mean? Doubtless, the Loring family loved Simeon. His gravestone in Sudbury's Revolutionary Cemetery states that Simeon was "the faithful and beloved servant of Israel Loring." But what did freedom mean for Simeon and Hannah, who, while no longer enslaved, would most likely continue to serve the same master and remain in the only household they had ever known? For most freed people, there were few opportunities to move on. Hannah, it is known, remained in the Loring house even after being emancipated, as indicated by the change from "Negro maid servant" to "hired woman servant." Whatever payment she might have received, the relationship had clearly changed even though her chores might have remained the same.

Perhaps the world they lived in—where slavery was accepted and fair treatment rare—a well-meaning master, who permitted mother and son to live together, was the best they could hope for.

Portsmouth and Ezekiel Howe

Ezekiel Howe came from one of the oldest families in Sudbury and adjacent Marlborough. In the mid-1700s, he took over from his father as innkeeper of Howe's Tavern in Sudbury and renamed it the Red Horse Tavern.[26] Later, it became known as The Wayside Inn, erasing the Howe family name but not its rich heritage. Howe also earned the title of colonel from his service with the Massachusetts Militia in the Revolutionary War, leading a company to Concord at the war's inception on April 19, 1775.

In 1840, Ezekiel Howe's granddaughter Jerusha How, known as the "Belle of Sudbury," recorded in her diary memories of Portsmouth or "Ponto," as he was called, a family slave:

The Negro man, who took care of me when a young child, and to whom I became very much attached, was purchased by Ezekiel How my grandfather of Mr. Wm. Baldwin of Sudbury administrator of the estate of Capt. Reynolds Seager for forty four pounds lawfull [sic] *money the 8th day of April 1773. The instrument said he was then about 33 years of age but must have been older. Named Portsmouth* [word between "Portsmouth" and "Said" indecipherable] *Said he was stolen from the Guinea coast while at play with other children and carried aboard ship. he remembered screaming for his mother when the men took them one under each arm to carry off. He became an intelligent man, had acquired great knowledge of the Bible, could write very well, and was blest with a strong retentive memory.*[27]

The original bill of sale in The Wayside Inn Archives verifies the accuracy of Jerusha How's information, despite the fact that she was only two years old when Portsmouth died. Portsmouth had previously been owned for an unknown period of time by Captain Reynolds Seager of Sudbury, who died in 1769. The sale of Portsmouth was part of the settlement of his estate.

Stories have long been associated with Portsmouth's life with the Howes; many lack documentation.[28] Portsmouth was said to have been a dwarf who slept in the attic on a bunk and was known to hide under a hallway shelf when visitors with whom he was not already familiar came calling. Portsmouth was also said to have refused his freedom when Howe offered it.

The Wayside Inn in Sudbury was the home of Colonel Ezekiel Howe, his enslaved man Portsmouth and at least one other enslaved person. *Painting by Alfred Sereno Hudson (1839–1907), courtesy of the Goodnow Library, Sudbury.*

Know all Men by these presents, that I William Baldwin of Sudbury in the County of Middlesex and Province of the Massachusetts Bay in New England Esq.... and Admr. of the Estate of Capt. Reynolds Seager Deceased for and in consideration of the sum of forty four pounds Lawful Money to me in hand before the ensealing and Delivery hereof well and truly paid by Ezekiel How of Sudbury in the County and Province aforesaid Gent.... the receipt whereof I hereby Acknowledge and thereof do Acquit and discharge the said Ezekiel How his Heirs and Assigns forever have given granted Bargained and Sold, and by these Presents do fully and absolutely, give Grant Bargain and Sell unto the said Ezekiel How his Heirs and Assigns forever a Negro Man Named Portsmouth aged about thirty three Years who Belonged to the Estate of Capt. Reynolds Seager Deced. to have and to hold the said Negro Man unto the said Ezekiel How his Heirs and Assigns forever to his and their own proper Use Benefit and Behoof forever and for myself my Heirs do hereby Covenant Promise Grant and Agree to Warrant and defend the said Negro Man Portsmouth unto the said Ezekiel How his Heirs and Assigns forever against the Lawful Claims and Demands of all Persons — In Witness whereof I have hereunto set my hand and Seal this Eighth Day of April Anno Domini 1773 in the Thirteenth Year of his Majesty's Reign.

Signed Sealed & Delivered in presence of

John Felton
Aaron Haynes

William Baldwin

Sale of Portsmouth from the estate of Captain Reynolds Seager to Colonel Ezekiel Howe in 1773. *Original in The Wayside Inn Archives and Research Center, Sudbury.*

Sketch made in 1891 by Arthur A. Shurtleff of Portsmouth's sleeping quarters in the attic. *Courtesy of The Wayside Inn Archives and Research Center, Sudbury.*

In the first federal census in 1790, Colonel Howe was listed as having two people of color living with him and no enslaved persons. As mentioned previously, in 1779, Howe purchased "a Negro Garll [*sic*]" in Boston, the last known sale of an enslaved person in Sudbury, which most likely accounts for the second person listed in the census.

Portsmouth was not listed in Howe's probate inventory, dated 1796, as he would have been if enslaved, but he was specifically mentioned in the codicil to the will:

> *My will is that my old Negro servant Portsmouth shall be subject to the orders of my wife...in such matters and things as be necessary to her about her household concerns and said servant shall be well and comfortably supported through life, both in sickness and health with all things suitable and necessary for a person of his age and quality and after his decease be buried in decent and Christian burial.*[29]

While the codicil has often been looked upon as a benevolent act by a caring master, Portsmouth, now free, was still expected to care for the family as a stipulation of his support. According to Lauren Prescott, archivist at

The Wayside Inn, Portsmouth died in 1799 and was buried on April 26. As of this writing, no grave has been located. The legends certainly support the theory that Portsmouth found comfort in the Howe household, yet it is obvious that he never forgot his home in Africa, or else Jerusha How would not have included it in her memories so many years after the fact.

THE DARK SIDE: A TALE OF TWO JOSIAH BROWNS

The treatment of enslaved persons varied in individual households, which makes it impossible to generalize. Puritan society was very hierarchical, and "slavery, although an extreme and uniquely violent form of subjugation," according to Professor Jarod Ross Hardesty, "existed alongside more traditional forms of bondage such as indentured servitude, apprenticeship, and marriage."[30] Yet sometimes, even snippets of information can indicate a troubled home. Could slaves be beaten? We only have to look back to the court case of Benjamin Crane and his enslaved boy to know they could be and were. Puritans were known for their "spare the rod and spoil the child" philosophy, as well as the use of the stocks, the ducking stool and other humiliating devices and punishments that were meted out to both whites and persons of color.

In Reverend Loring's *Journal* for 1729, we find an intriguing entry without any further comment: "Heard of the sad accident fallen out in the family of Mr. Josiah Brown. His Negro man servant dangerously wounding himself by a gun, which he designedly discharged against himself, both shot and wadding went into his body."

In 1743, mistreatment of another enslaved person in Josiah Brown's household may be the reason behind the only documented ad for a runaway slave from Sudbury:

Run-away from Josiah Browne [sic] *of Sudbury, on the 6ᵗʰ Day of June Instant, A Negro Man named Sampson, about 23 Years of Age; middling Stature; has a pretty large Leg; walks light & Spritely on the Ground; Had on when he went away, a Castor Hat, a Cap, a dark coloured Coat all Wool, with plain white Metal Buttons, a blue Cloth Jacket, with brass Buttons filled with Wood & Catgut Eyes, a Cotton & Linnin* [linen] *Shirt, Leather Breeches, white cotton Stockings, a pair of double-fol'd turned Pumps; and took with him a Pair of large Silver Buckles, a dark colour'd Silk Handkerchief. Whoever shall take up said Run-away and him safely convey to his above said Master at Sudbury, shall have Five Pounds old Tenor Reward.*[31]

These are almost certainly two different enslaved males. If Sampson's age was correctly reported in 1743, he would have been a child in 1729 and, therefore, was not the same "Negro man servant" who tried to end his own life fourteen years earlier.

Confusion arises because there were two Josiah Browns who lived in Sudbury during this period, complicated by the fact that a number of online resources conflate the two men. Both appear to have served in the French and Indian War. Which Josiah Brown is the master of the enslaved persons in these two instances is uncertain, but there is a strong possibility that it was not the Josiah Brown who referred to himself as a yeoman (farmer) and left little of value when he died in 1774. The more likely Josiah Brown was one of the most prominent and prosperous men in town, son of Hopestill Brown, a slaveowner. He was a large landowner and an active churchgoer who signed the original covenant when the west-side parish was set up in 1724–25. He held almost every town office and donated land to the West Side Church. He was referred to as Colonel Brown after his service in the French and Indian War in the 1750s, but when the attempted suicide of his "Negro man" occurred in 1729, Reverend Loring referred to him as "Mister" Josiah Brown because it preceded his military service. According to West Side Church records and Reverend Loring's *Journal*, Colonel Josiah Brown owned at least two enslaved men in his later years.[32] When he died in 1762, he left everything in his will to his "beloved wife," Beulah, without itemizing bequests individually in an inventory. In 1763, Mrs. Brown was listed as the owner of Caesar when he became a member of the West Side Church.

Not surprisingly, few reports of cruelty have been recorded in extant family histories. We can only imagine how many more incidents like this there might have been in a quiet Puritan village.

Chapter 4

THE PERSONAL LIFE OF PROPERTY

In social interactions of people of color with one another and with whites, the human need for personal relationships posed new challenges for the enslaved. With only one or, at most, two enslaved people per family and restrictions on mobility, most lived on the bottom rung of an all-white household. No enslaved person had the freedom to control his social circle or live in an environment where his social interactions were not subject to his owner's control.

Nowhere was this isolation more evident than in marriages. Professor Lorenzo Greene in *The Negro in Colonial New England* devoted a chapter to the marriages of enslaved persons.[33] Unlike the South, where enslaved couples were forbidden to marry, Puritan owners permitted marriage with their consent. Sex without marriage was frowned upon in Puritan New England, despite its frequency, no matter whether you were enslaved or free. What might seem an acknowledgement of a slave's humanity was in reality clouded by restrictive laws and the control of their masters. It must be remembered that in the best cases, marriage among whites provided almost no privileges to women, but slave marriages went well beyond even that inequity. Despite claims by the masters regarding those held in bondage as "family," many differences were evident in the rules that governed white families and Black families who were enslaved.

Enslaved couples assumed no surnames upon marriage, nor were they known as "Mr." and "Mrs." Occasionally, the last name of the master was used to record a marriage. In 1762, when Cuff and Hagar married, they were given the last name "Noyes" since both were then enslaved by Colonel

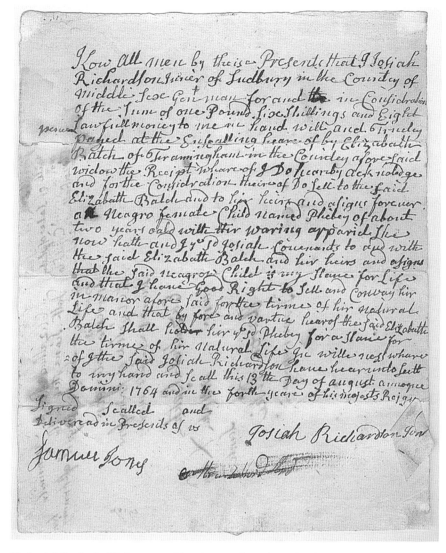

Phebey's bill of sale. Phebey was sold at the age of two by Josiah Richardson Jr. of Sudbury to the widow Balch of Framingham. *Courtesy of Framingham History Center Collection.*

John Noyes. However, they were not listed in the marriage records of other members of the Noyes family but at the end in a section entitled "Negroes."

Married slaves remained the property of their respective masters and were subject to their authority. They did not live together but remained in the households of their owners, even in separate towns from one another. Childbearing was not encouraged, but if any children were born to enslaved couples, they became the property of the mother's owner. Unlike in the South, where more hands were needed for year-round agricultural production, owners of enslaved mothers regarded the child as another mouth to feed. A child might distract the enslaved mother from her work for her owner's family, without the advantage of providing useful labor until the child was older.

Parental decisions lay not with the enslaved parents but with the masters. Unwanted children of slaves could be sold, as happened in Sudbury in 1764.

The Framingham History Center has the bill of sale for Phebey, a "negro female child" about two years old, enslaved by Josiah Richardson Jr. of Sudbury.[34] She was sold to the widow Balch of Framingham for £1.6.8. No information about the identity of Phebey's mother or father has yet been discovered. We don't even know whether her mother was alive or dead. In fact, many slave children were sold while young so that they could be raised in the families they would serve when old enough to work. At the time of Phebey's sale, Josiah Jr.'s father, Josiah Richardson Sr., also owned an enslaved child, Cesar, who remained in the Richardson household with his enslaved mother, Dinah.

Dinah had married Cesar, servant of Mrs. Love Flint of Lincoln, in 1761. When their child Cesar, presumably named after his father, was born in 1762, he lived with the Richardson family.[35] Father Cesar remained in Lincoln enslaved by Mrs. Flint, but not for long. He died only four days after the birth of his son, leaving Dinah as the sole parent.

Economic considerations might result in the breakup of the slave family at any time. Enslaved husbands and wives could be sold or given to new masters individually, as happened to the slaves of the Reverend John Swift of Framingham when he died in 1745.[36] In his will, Reverend Swift broke up a married couple, Nero and Dido Benson. Nero was left to Reverend Swift's son-in-law, Dr. Ebenezer Roby of Sudbury, while Dido and their daughter remained with the widow Swift in Framingham. Their son Francis or Frank, as he was sometimes called, believed to be about twenty-three years of age, became the property of Reverend Swift's son and namesake, the minister in Acton. Reverend John Swift of Acton soon sold Frank to Josiah Richardson Sr. of Sudbury.

Some slave couples did live together—for example, Colonel Noyes's Cuff and Hagar. But they could only do so until Colonel Noyes decided to sell one or both or until he died and divided them in his will. There was no option for enslaved married couples and their children to live in as a family of their own or even guarantee that they would not be separated.

Chapter 5

SLAVERY AND THE
CONGREGATIONAL CHURCH[37]

The Congregational Church was not the only church in New England to admit enslaved Africans and other persons of color; the Anglican Church and others did as well. However, since the Congregational Church was the only denomination in Sudbury, which remained a quintessential Puritan village throughout the colonial period, all mentions of the Church in Sudbury refer to it.

Puritan ministers walked a fine line to justify enslavement and, at the same time, encourage enslaved persons to become Christians without offering manumission. In New England, African Americans, either enslaved or free, could attend white churches, participate in some church rituals and even become full members. They took part in prayer and singing. Although a rare occurrence, enslaved persons could transfer from one church to another, as described in the upcoming section on Nero Benson. African Americans were segregated in seating in the church; how much this was due to social status rather than color is unclear. As discussed earlier, the Church did not offer equality to Black people, only a hope of possible redemption and a way to serve their masters and God with proper guidance and resignation. According to Dr. Kenneth Minkema of Yale Divinity School, "There was a hierarchy in the Church as well as in all other facets of colonial life for African Americans and restrictions to their participation did apply."[38]

In colonial Sudbury, enslaved men and women appear in church records of baptisms, membership and most frequently for "owning the covenant," also known as halfway membership. Professor Richard J. Boles, who did

Artist's rendering of the first meetinghouse/church built on the west side of the Sudbury River after the town divided into two precincts in the early 1720s. *Painting by Alfred Sereno Hudson (1839–1907), courtesy of the Goodnow Library, Sudbury.*

a comprehensive study of the relationship of persons of color and New England denominations, asserts that by owning the covenant, a simple statement of faith, you were affirming your understanding of and belief in the doctrines of Christianity and submitting to the oversight and discipline of the church members. "Despite its limitations," he noted, "owning the covenant or halfway membership provided a formal place in church life and the community, and not a few blacks [*sic*] and Indians owned the covenant to receive baptism."[39]

Full membership was rare in Sudbury and not to be undertaken lightly, as it required sharing religious testimony with the congregation. Only full members could take communion and, in some instances, vote in church affairs. Only Nero Benson and two other enslaved persons are mentioned as full members in existing church records for Sudbury.

The motivations of enslaved churchgoers have been the subject of much speculation, and no doubt the reasons varied from one individual to another. How much was due to forced attendance by owners rather than by choice is also uncertain. In *Dividing the Faith*, Professor Boles explained some of the possible reasons why church affiliation would appeal to enslaved and marginalized persons:

Often, both material and spiritual motivations were present for the blacks [sic] and Indians who participated in these churches. Church services were opportunities to see other enslaved friends and family members dispersed across the town. Some churches provided educational opportunities that blacks [sic] and whites sought after. In these contexts, being a church member carried a degree of social status, and Christianity could provide a positive identity for enslaved and dispossessed people.[40]

In short, Professor Boles concludes that "available written accounts suggest that Christianity could be comforting, empowering, or life-enriching to some blacks [sic] and Indians, just as it was to some whites."[41]

While some enslaved persons responded to the call to become Christians, many did not. For those who did, no one illustrates the central role of the Church in the life of a person of color more than Nero Benson.

NERO BENSON AND THE REVEREND ISRAEL LORING

While we know more about Nero Benson than about any other enslaved person in colonial Sudbury, so much more lies beneath the surface. What a wealth of lived experiences we would have if only Nero had written down something about his own life, and it is almost certain that he could read and write. Probably unwritten, or possibly missing, there is an overwhelming message: nothing we know about African Americans in Sudbury was written from their point of view. Even in secondhand accounts, it is easy to imagine Nero as a unique individual yearning for freedom with strong convictions and an indomitable will.

Nero was the patriarch of the Benson family, one of the few African American families that not only had a last name but also one that differed from its known owners. Nero's life is thought to have begun in Africa, but it is in Framingham, Massachusetts, where his recorded history begins. As mentioned earlier, Nero Benson was enslaved by Reverend John Swift, the first minister of neighboring Framingham. Nero was known for his musical skill, so much so that in 1725, he was trumpeter in Captain Isaac Clark's Massachusetts militia troop. Later, his grandson Abel Benson of Framingham served as a trumpeter in the Revolutionary War, possibly using Nero's trumpet. By 1725, Nero was also a married man, as noted in the vital records of the town of Framingham. In 1721, Nero married Dido Dingo (later known as Dido Benson), also enslaved by Reverend Swift of

Framingham and also believed to be a native of Africa. While still enslaved in 1737, Nero made application to and was received into the church in nearby Hopkinton, Massachusetts, as were a number of white church members who, like Nero, had previously been part of Reverend Swift's congregation. This was apparently precipitated by the arrival of Captain Edward Goddard from Boston to Framingham and his contention that ruling elders should govern the church. Reverend Swift disagreed. Goddard's followers, including Nero, still enslaved by the Framingham minister, seceded and joined the Hopkinton Church.

This was obviously not a hasty decision on Nero's part. In 1736, Nero had written a letter to Reverend Loring in Sudbury (most likely his first interaction with his future chronicler) asking him to intervene in this matter. According to Reverend Loring's *Journal*, the letter was read at the West Parish Church, and "after some debate…, it was voted that the affair should be dismissed."[42] While this appears to be Nero's first foray into issues over church doctrine, it would not be his last. The Church played a major role throughout the rest of Nero Benson's life and was the primary reason that we hear so much about him in Reverend Loring's *Journals*.

As previously noted, when Reverend Swift died in 1745, his five slaves were divided in his will. Nero was left to Dr. Ebenezer Roby of Sudbury, Reverend Swift's son-in-law, while Dido Benson remained with Mrs. Swift in Framingham. Dr. Roby did not keep Nero for long, although he had other enslaved persons in his household during his lifetime; one was listed in the inventory of his will when he died in 1772. By 1747, Nero had been sold to a Sudbury man named Samuel Wood, who gave Nero his freedom. His emancipation, which still remains in the record books in the Sudbury town clerk's office, declared: "The said Nero Benson is absolutely a free man and fully set at liberty from all slavery whatsoever by or under me."

Emancipation meant that Samuel Wood, his former owner, agreed to pay for the support of Nero Benson if he ever became a town charge. According to Judge A. Leon Higginbotham in *In the Matter of Color: Race & the American Legal Process*, "[Massachusetts] did impose some limits on a master's ability to manumit his slaves through legislation passed in 1703." This act, requiring masters to post security before freeing their slaves, was ostensibly caused by the "great charge and inconveniences…to divers towns and places' occasioned by the practice of freeing old or ill unskilled slaves who were unable to support themselves and thus had to be supported by the towns."[43] Wood paid the Town of Sudbury a bond of £100 (only £50 was required by law) "to indemnify and save the town harmless from

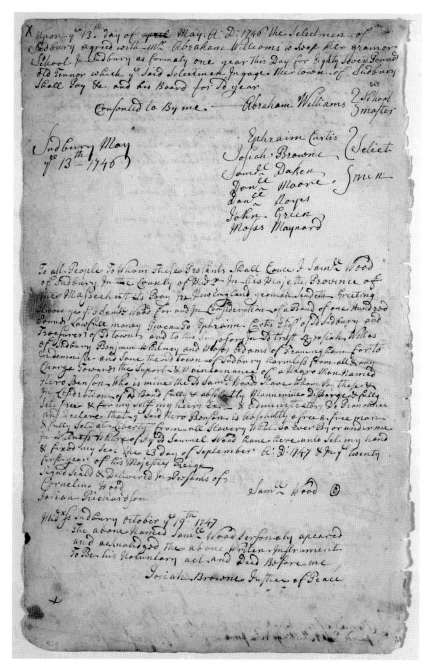

Declaration of Emancipation from Slavery for Nero Benson and Surety Bond by his owner, Samuel Wood, guaranteeing that Nero Benson would not become a town charge. As of this writing, it is the only documented freedom paper in colonial Sudbury. *Courtesy of the Town Clerk's Office, Sudbury.*

all and any charges towards the support and maintenance of a Negro man named Nero Benson." The surety bond guaranteed that the Town of Sudbury would incur no expenses for his care, including lodging, food, clothing and medical treatments.

Why was Nero Benson emancipated? His emancipation is the only one recorded for an enslaved person who lived in Sudbury. What were the elusive characteristics that made Dr. Roby quickly sell Nero Benson and caused Samuel Wood to free him? Often, we look for clues in attitudes that favored emancipation. But this is harder to do in Nero's case. Not only did Dr. Roby own slaves, but it appears that Samuel Wood did as well and very likely at the same time he freed Nero. Two years after Nero's emancipation, William, "Negro" servant of Samuel Wood, accepted the church covenant of Reverend Loring's church on the west side. What qualities did Nero possess that made his owners in colonial Sudbury find him unfit for bondage? Clearly, Nero had a mind of his own and a profound effect on the people who owned him. His religious devotion, although undocumented in his emancipation, may also have been a factor. Almost a year before Nero Benson became a freed man, he was accepted as a full member in Reverend Loring's church.[44] As you may recall, Nero had previously joined churches in Framingham and Hopkinton before his arrival in Sudbury in 1745.

By 1753, Nero, no longer enslaved, was back in Reverend Loring's *Journal*. He and another member of the church, Cornelius Wood, the brother of his emancipator Samuel, were embroiled in a dispute. Without specifying the nature of the disagreement, the matter was settled when Nero Benson acknowledged that he had "wronged Cornelius Wood in reporting that [Wood] had taken a false oath." Reverend Loring was clearly relieved and thanked God for settling "the unhappy differences between Cornelius Wood and Nero Benson which endangered still wider breaches in the Church." It is obvious that not only was the Church important to Nero Benson, but Nero Benson was important to the Church as well.[45]

One last entry on Nero Benson from Reverend Loring's *Journal* is dated July 4, 1757: "This day attended the funeral of Nero Benson who died at the schoolhouse July 3rd Lord's Day. A Negro, and admitted into the Church here Nov. 9, 1746. Left behind him a Widow and three children."

Perhaps the funeral, held on July 4, which later became Independence Day, serves to remind us of Nero Benson's love of freedom at a time when very little external reward was offered to persons of color. Even in death, Black people remained segregated. Some gravestones that remain in New England cemeteries offer flowery tributes confirming Lorenzo Greene's assertion in *The Negro in Colonial New England* that "the slave in death sometimes received a recognition which was denied him in life." While this might be true in general, as of this writing, only three graves in modern Wayland and Sudbury can be documented as belonging to enslaved persons: Simeon's grave in Revolutionary Cemetery in Sudbury and Peter Booz and Flora in Wayland's North Cemetery. Presumably many others, like Nero Benson, are buried in unmarked graves.

Chapter 6

TWO FAMILIES OF COLOR

The Bensons and Harrys of Sudbury and Framingham

DIDO DINGO BENSON

Nero's widow, Dido Dingo Benson, has also been recorded in colonial Sudbury but in a very different way. In 1745, Dido was bequeathed to Reverend Swift's wife, Sarah, and after her death to her daughter Martha. Sarah died in 1747 and Martha two years later, and Dido presumably remained in Framingham, where her owners lived. Though this fact is lacking any discovered documentation, Dido had undoubtedly been freed at some point before 1757 or she would not have been allowed to travel from town to town. It is likely that at some point she joined Nero in Sudbury, though when or where they lived is unknown. Soon after Nero's death, the warrant for Town Meeting on October 6, 1757, sought "to see what the Town will do, with respect to Dido, A Negro Woman who is now upon Charge, in this Town." Dido had no means to support herself. When the meeting convened a few weeks later, "The Town by their Vote Ordered the Select Men of Sudbury, to make strict enquiry who brought Dido into Town."

After a lifetime of service to others, Dido belonged to that large group of freed people, especially older women, without a place to call home and with few chances to earn income to provide for her own needs. It is not known when Dido left Sudbury, but it was not the only town where she was told to leave because she did not belong there, a practice known as "warning out." In 1762, Dido was warned out of Shrewsbury, Massachusetts, in Worcester County, along with her son, William, and his white wife.[46]

Warning out, like posting a surety bond for emancipating a slave by a master, was another way for the town to avoid paying any expenses for people whom they regarded as not belonging. Unlike manumitting a slave, warning out applied to all persons, Black, white or Indigenous, whom the town considered to be outsiders ("strangers"). Warning out did not necessarily mean removal from a town so much as a declaration that the town was not financially responsible for their care. Towns of one's birth had a legal obligation to care for indigent persons, but this posed greater challenges if you had been enslaved. This was especially so for those, like Dido, who had been imported from the West Indies or Africa or were removed from their birthplace while too young to remember. Once the matter of the legal residence was resolved, that town was expected to pay any costs, including room and board, clothing and medical expenses, that the indigent person had incurred while cared for by the other town.

By 1763, Dido was back in Sudbury, which indicates that Sudbury took responsibility for her, although there are no known records on how the decision was made. In 1763, Samuel Puffer Jr. was reimbursed by the town for a pair of shoes for Dido Benson,[47] and in 1764, Jabez Puffer was reimbursed for boarding Dido and making a bed for her "to lie on from December to the following spring," indicating that the town was now assuming responsibility for her expenses.[48] Thereafter, she disappears from available written records. Her date of death and place of residence at the time of her death are unknown, as is her burial site.

FRANCIS "FRANK" BENSON

In contrast to his father, Nero, Francis Benson's life involves sojourns in four nearby communities west of Boston. And to add to the confusion, records indicate that Francis was also interchangeably known as Frank. The last name Benson never changed, but at times it may have been omitted when referring to him. And whereas we know a good deal about Nero Benson from Reverend Loring's *Journals*, most of the records for Francis Benson come from more impersonal sources that list only the event and his name.

Francis Benson's journey from his birthplace in Framingham to Sudbury began in 1745, when his enslaver, the Reverend John Swift, died and left Francis to his son and namesake, the minister of Acton. Reverend John Swift of Acton almost immediately sold him to Josiah Richardson Sr. of Sudbury.[49] It seems safe to assume that Francis primarily served the needs of

Josiah Richardson Sr. and the male members of his family, as Josiah's wife, Experience Wight Richardson, never referred to him in the diary she kept for most of her adult life. In 1749, Francis Benson accepted the covenant of Reverend Loring's West Side Church three years after his father became a member.[50] In 1761, Francis Benson, still enslaved, married Hannah Harry, almost certainly the same woman once enslaved by Reverend Loring but now freed.[51] Both Francis Benson and Hannah Harry lived in Sudbury, where it is almost certain that Francis remained in the Richardson household, while Hannah's dwelling place is unknown but can be presumed to be the Loring household. Experience Richardson makes no mention of Hannah's presence in her family home. Francis remained enslaved when Josiah Richardson Sr. died in 1770;[52] he was left to Josiah Richardson's son, Josiah Jr., also of Sudbury. Hannah Harry died in Sudbury in 1774,[53] and it is uncertain whether her husband was still in town at that time.

In 1775, at the start of the American Revolution, an enslaved man named Frank entered the diaries and letters of Concord's minister, the Reverend William Emerson. Although he was never referred to as Frank or Francis Benson (only Frank) in Emerson's letters, historians of Concord in the Revolutionary War period who have studied enslavement, such as Dr. Robert Gross, author of *The Minutemen and Their World*, have concluded that almost certainly Frank and Frank Benson are one and the same.[54] *The Diaries and Letters of William Emerson 1743–1776* place Frank at the Old Manse, the Emerson home next to Concord's North Bridge, on April 19, 1775, the first day of the American Revolution. The diaries follow Frank's service to Reverend Emerson through Emerson's time as a chaplain in the Revolutionary army and Emerson's death in 1776 returning from his post at Fort Ticonderoga in New York. Additional information was provided by Amelia Forbes Emerson, a direct descendant, who edited Reverend Emerson's diaries and letters and published them in 1972. She wrote that Frank was still enslaved at the time of Reverend Emerson's death and was freed, along with his other enslaved persons, on his deathbed in 1776.[55] By 1777, when Rosanna Lewis married Frank Benson in Concord, they are listed as "both Negros," making the connection to Emerson's enslaved man named Frank even stronger and his freed status likely.

But how does that connect Frank Benson to Sudbury, the focus of this study, where he was almost exclusively known as Francis Benson? On December 28, 1779, Rosanna and Frank Benson had a daughter, Hannah Harry Benson, in Concord, presumably named after Frank's first wife. Almost certainly, Frank Benson and Francis Benson are the same person.

Bill of Sale for Frank Benson from Reverend John Swift of Acton to Josiah Richardson Sr. of Sudbury. *Courtesy of the Stearns Collection, Goodnow Library.*

Later, we will look at the related Harry family of Sudbury and Framingham, another complex family that, like Frank Benson, had a penchant for using and reusing the same first names.

Tax records place Frank Benson in Concord in 1780,[56] when his name appeared on a tax list, after which he disappeared from the town's records.

As a freeman, Benson would be assessed a poll tax, or head tax, levied on every male who resided in the town age sixteen and older, irrespective of race or status. Inexplicably, his name appeared on that list even though he was the only individual on it who was not assigned a monetary amount for his poll tax; that column was left blank. After colonial Sudbury divided in 1780, a Francis Benson was assessed a poll tax in East Sudbury in the years 1783 and 1784,[57] meaning that he was a resident of the town at that time. The last reference we have to Francis Benson in East Sudbury is a Town Meeting appropriation paying him for road work in 1787.[58] Currently, there are no documents that account for his removal to the west (Sudbury) side, and his name does not appear in Sudbury's Assessor's Records. In fact, unlike in East Sudbury, in Sudbury, as of this writing, no African American names are listed on the tax rolls in the 1780s or 1790s, although Portsmouth, formerly enslaved by Ezekiel Howe, is known to have remained in Sudbury until his death in 1799.

At some point, Francis Benson presumably returned to Sudbury with Rosanna, who was apparently now known as Rose. No other Frank or Francis Benson is recorded in the town or vital records during this time. His death date is thus far undiscovered but can be documented as occurring before 1803, as there is another story left to tell involving once again the towns of Concord and Sudbury. It is the story of Rose Benson at the end of her life.

Rosanna "Rose" Benson

While occurring after slavery ended in Massachusetts, what happened to Rose Benson serves as another poignant reminder of the limitations of freedom for a person of color.

Presumed to be the same person as the previously described Rosanna Benson, by 1802 she appears in the Poor Records of the Town of Concord.[59] While little is known about her life before her marriage to Frank Benson, at the end of her life, Rose—like her mother-in-law, Dido, earlier—suffered not only all the deprivations of most woman and widows in the early Republic but also the callous treatment of persons of color. Few, if any, opportunities existed to make a living, own property or pay medical expenses.

According to records in the town clerk's office in Concord, in January 1803, the selectmen of Sudbury replied to a request from the overseers of the poor of Concord, where Rose was residing, to pay for her care, as Concord considered Sudbury "her legal place of settlement." The selectmen of

Sudbury wrote that "we should be willing to make provision for her support where she now is or carry immediate removal to take place, but we are very certain that the legal place of settlement of Rose Benson is not in the Town of Sudbury." As with her mother-in-law, Dido Benson, who had been warned out of Sudbury and Shrewsbury earlier, the Town of Concord was making it known that it was not responsible for Rose's care, as it did not consider her a legal resident. The little we know of Rose's recorded history, her marriage to Frank Benson and the birth of their child, certainly puts her in Concord, but we do not know where she was born, whether she had been enslaved or whether she had any personal connection to colonial Sudbury apart from her husband. Despite Sudbury's initial ambivalence to Concord's letter, by April 4, 1803, Sudbury's Town Meeting had agreed to pay Concord for her support.[60] Sudbury was presented an itemized bill that included wood, meat, meal, bread, sugar, molasses and candles. The cost of shelter, nursing care and medicine also was charged to Sudbury. Before her death in June 1803,[61] Rose was returned to Sudbury, her presumed legal settlement. Her death, as reported in the burial records of the Sudbury Church, merely recorded her as "a Negro, widow of Frank Benson," telling us that her husband had already died.

Despite the written records, there are a number of unanswered questions. When and where did Rose Benson live in Sudbury considering that the town agreed to pay for her? After Frank died, if indeed he died in Sudbury, it is reasonable that Rose would return to Concord, where her daughter Hannah most likely lived, as she married there in 1804. So far, no public records have surfaced that explain the presence of Frank and Rose Benson in Sudbury. Yet acceptance of legal residency was not taken lightly, as it was a substantial expense to a small town. And most of all, what did freedom mean to someone who spent her final moments as the source of a dispute between two towns that clearly did not want her?

HARRY FAMILY OF SUDBURY AND FRAMINGHAM

The history of the Harry family of Sudbury and Framingham presents an intricate puzzle with pieces scattered in many different places. It is not until enough pieces are assembled that one can make reasonable claims as to what the final picture is, including its connection to the Benson family.

In 1714 and 1716, Henry and Frances Harry had two sons, Simeon and Peter, whose births were recorded in the Sudbury Vital Records. There was

The Harry Family of Sudbury and Framingham

Harry family chart highlights the multiple uses of the same first names. *Designed by the author and Ashley Sciacca.*

no designation of their race or status. It is only at a later date that we discover that they were Black. As referred to in an earlier chapter, another Simeon, born circa 1734, enters the scene as "born and brought up" in the Loring household. Reverend Loring never referred to his enslaved boy Simeon with a last name in his journal entries, but on June 20, 1741, he recorded, "Simeon Harry a Negro was with me to desire baptism for himself. A person of Good knowledge declaring that he has been under awakenings by my late preaching." Almost certainly, this is the Simeon Harry who was born in Sudbury in 1714 and was now living in Framingham, the adjacent town, and not seven-year-old Simeon who lived with the Lorings. The following month, Peter Harry, Simeon Harry's brother, came to see Reverend Loring for the same purpose. Simeon Harry did "own the covenant" and worshipped at the West Side Church later that year, but Peter Harry did not; he died in Sudbury in 1745.

Reverend Loring also had an enslaved maidservant named Hannah, detailed in an earlier chapter. Before young Simeon's death at the age of twenty-one in 1755, Hannah had been set free, according to Reverend Loring's *Journal*, but remained in the Loring household as a hired maid. Could she be the one who was called Hannah Harry when she married Francis Benson in Sudbury in 1761? Again, Hannah had not been referred to as anything but Hannah in Loring's journals. To add to the confusion, Simeon Harry of Framingham had four children between 1754 and 1761; one was named Hannah, another one was named Peter and a third was named Simeon after himself (the fourth child was Rubin). So that could account for Hannah Harry marrying Francis Benson in 1761, as related in some histories, if only she wasn't seven years old.

More of the puzzle comes together with young Simeon's death in the Loring household in 1755 when Reverend Loring informs us that Hannah was Simeon's mother, and the recently deceased Susannah Harry was her sister. Around the same time, another piece fell into place in Dr. Ebenezer Roby's account books from 1749 to 1764, held at Harvard's Francis A. Countway Library of Medicine. Dr. Roby of Sudbury attended Susannah Harry in Framingham before her 1755 death in the household of "Sim [Simeon] Harry Negro" and identified Susannah as his sister. If Hannah and Susannah were sisters and Simeon Harry and Susannah were brother and sister, then Simeon Harry was also Hannah's brother and the uncle of young Simeon.

It seems reasonable to make several assumptions at this point. When Simeon Harry and Peter Harry were born in Sudbury in 1714 and 1716, their births were recorded, but those of their sisters, Hannah and Susannah, were not. This is plausible when we consider the status of females in colonial New England. Hannah, maidservant to the Lorings, was indeed Hannah Harry and certainly could have used that last name when she married Francis Benson in 1761. In her burial record on May 1, 1774, she is listed as "Hannah, wife of Francis Benson." Hannah undoubtedly would have been older than her husband, but when you consider that they lived in a very proscribed area with few mates to choose from, that is not all that surprising. It is obvious that their marriage was meaningful enough for Francis to name his daughter after her when he remarried and had a child.

One puzzle piece is still missing. While we know more about the status of the Benson family, the only members of the Harry family who can be documented as enslaved were those who belonged to Reverend Loring: Hannah and young Simeon.

Chapter 7

THE IMPERSONAL LIFE OF
PERSONS OF COLOR

Primary Source Record

As mentioned previously, Puritans almost without exception referred to all who served them, including those enslaved, as "servants." The word "slave" was not commonly used to describe the status of enslaved persons in New England, and indeed, some fall into a gray area, probably enslaved without documented proof. More documented records exist for colonial Sudbury that emphasize enslaved persons' value as property than exist of their personhood. In addition to the information found in this section, a full list for each category will appear in the appendix. As of this writing, over thirty slaveowners and more than fifty enslaved persons can be documented as living in Sudbury during the late seventeenth and eighteenth centuries.

THE UPSIDE AND DOWNSIDE OF HUMAN RIGHTS OF PROPERTY: THE LAW[62]

Enslaved persons daily confronted a duality in their personal lives, being regarded as both persons and property. Deciphering all the ins and outs of the legal system no doubt posed a challenge to all residents of Massachusetts regardless of race or status. The laws governing the enslaved are at the forefront of this confusion. As will be addressed later, enslaved persons were restricted by law from a great many of the privileges of white townsmen, but when it involved the court system, it was less so. As Professor Jared Ross Hardesty explains:

> *Unlike plantation colonies in the American South and Caribbean, the New England colonies did not create special slave courts or bar people of color from testifying in court. Instead they used the same courts as white colonists and could be called as witnesses, offer testimony, file petitions, and even be plaintiffs against whites.*[63]

That is not to imply that discrimination did not occur in the court system, as those who judged them were white, but that there was a recognition of humanity. This did not apply to other interactions of enslaved persons in legal affairs.

As detailed in Lorenzo Greene's chapter titled "Machinery of Control," a series of laws were enacted in the eighteenth century in Massachusetts limiting almost all aspects of an enslaved person's life, imposing curfews and restricting drinking, marriage, movement and any activity deemed as "disturbing the peace." Punishments for violating these laws were also defined and carried out by local officials.

Many legal documents, such as emancipation papers and bills of sale, added to the dehumanization of those who were enslaved. Emancipation papers included a pledge of money by the owner to the town so it would not have to assume any expenses for those who were freed. The only emancipation paper discovered in Sudbury thus far is for Nero Benson, in which Samuel Wood posted a surety bond of £100 "to indemnifie [*sic*] and hold harmless the Town of Sudbury for maintenance of Nero Benson."

More bills of sale from colonial Sudbury have survived than emancipation decrees. The sale of Frank Benson to Josiah Richardson Sr. is in Sudbury's Goodnow Library, and two property deeds of purchases made by Ezekiel Howe for enslaved persons are in the Archives of The Wayside Inn. The Wayland Museum and Historical Society is home to a bill of sale for Cato from Colonel John Noyes to his son Jonas in 1767. The sale of Phebey by Josiah Richardson Jr. to a Framingham woman, as discussed earlier, is at the Framingham History Center. These deeds of sale were called "property deeds," underscoring the fact that these were legal monetary transactions benefiting the seller and purchaser of their human possessions.

What limitations to the life of an enslaved person not proscribed or granted by law were left to individual owners to decide. For example, enslaved persons in Massachusetts could own property. Few did, but it was

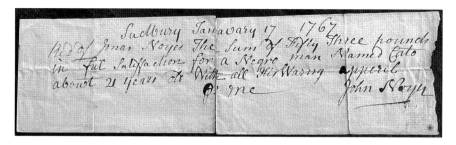

Sale of Cato by Colonel John Noyes to his son, Jonas Noyes, for fifty-three pounds. *Copy of the original courtesy of the Wayland Historical Society.*

not against the law. In rare instances, a master might sell or bequeath land to an enslaved person. So far, no enslaved property owners have been discovered in Sudbury, although they have been found in neighboring Weston.[64] Also, with the permission of their owners, enslaved persons could be hired out and earn wages and be allowed to keep a portion of their earnings. In some instances, especially during the turbulent years leading to the start of the Revolutionary War, enslaved persons with earned income used their personal funds as leverage to buy their freedom. As of this writing, there are no known instances of this happening in Sudbury.

Census Records and Tax Valuation Lists

Census records, often used in conjunction with tax records, are the best sources of hard evidence for an enslaved population, although they must be approached with caution.

Of the existing records, the Massachusetts Provincial Tax Valuation of 1771[65] is perhaps the best known, in which slaveowners had to report the number of their "servants for life." In it, 911 residents of the Bay Colony owned 1,169 "servants for life," including "Indian, negroes, molotto [*sic*], from ages 14 to 45." On that list, 12 slaveowners lived in Sudbury and were taxed for 1 slave each. The enslaved were not named, as it pertained to taxes that impacted only the owners. Noteworthy is the fact that any "servant for life" under fourteen or over forty-five was not included. This serves as a strong indicator of the presumed productive work life of those who were enslaved and gives the impression that 1 slave per family was the norm. If everyone had been counted, undoubtedly, the numbers would have increased. Additionally, for matters of taxation, slaveowners had a great incentive to undercount to save money.

A 1749 tax list for Sudbury still survives in very fragile condition in the Sudbury Town Clerk's vault and lists the number of enslaved persons as seventeen. If any names were included, they are no longer decipherable.

Even less enlightening is the 1754 so-called Slave Census, in which Governor William Shirley ordered that each town in the Province of Massachusetts Bay appoint assessors to report on the number of slaves in their town over the age of sixteen. Sudbury, one of the towns that complied with Shirley's order, reported nine males and five females.[66] No names of the owners or the enslaved were included.

A valuation list for Sudbury dated 1763, found in the Massachusetts Archive collection on Family Search, lists the number of "servants for life" as 11 in 263 households.[67]

All the figures thus far have been fairly consistent as to the number of enslaved living in Sudbury at any one time, ranging from twelve to seventeen. That, however, is not the case in the Lost Census of 1765.[68] No doubt "lost" amid the turmoil that led to the outbreak of the Revolutionary War in Massachusetts in 1775, its fascinating history is detailed in *Early Census Making in Massachusetts, 1743–1765* by Josiah H. Benton in 1905, available on various online sites. The census was first discovered in 1822 among the papers of a "deceased friend" of Judge Samuel Dana of Groton, Massachusetts, but other discoveries followed, as did challenges to the identity of the original finder.

In regard to enumerating African Americans, the 1765 report contained not only the number of enslaved people in each town but also the mood in the colony: "The free Negroes & Mulattos are very few.…The People here are very much tired of Negro Servants; and it is generally thought that it would be for the public good to discourage their Importation, if it was not at present very inconsiderable, not one Parcell [*sic*] having been imported this year as yet."[69]

Despite the commentary, Sudbury reported more "Negroes" than it ever had before or afterward, and there was no distinction between enslaved and free. There were fifteen males and twelve females for a total of twenty-seven. How could this be? One possible answer is that the count was transcribed incorrectly. Another might also be worth considering. Whereas white inhabitants were broken up into four separate counts— males and females under sixteen and those above sixteen—there was only one category for those who were Black in 1765. Unlike most other census records, there was no mention of excluding those above or below a certain age. If this was indeed an accurate number, there may have been far more persons who were Black in Sudbury who were never recorded. Tax lists and valuations tended to undercount the number of enslaved, so it remains an open question.

In 1777, a Massachusetts census reported 522 male inhabitants in Sudbury over the age of sixteen. There were 6 "Negroes" in town, with no distinction made between enslaved, free or freed or between male and female. No age range was specified. From the 1771 census, which listed 12 "servants for life between 14 and 45," the number had decreased by at least half. This was clearly a downward trend that would accelerate as the American War for Independence progressed.

In the first federal census in 1790, Massachusetts[70] was the only state that reported no enslaved persons. Sudbury and East Sudbury households listed eleven free persons of color, two in Sudbury and nine in East Sudbury. Almost all of these households were known to have formerly had enslaved persons living in them, and the likelihood is that some of those individuals were still there. In the same census, no persons of color were listed as property owners, nor were they listed as property owners in yearly tax valuations from the 1780s and 1790s.

Probate Records

Probate records often provide the names of the enslaved but little else in the way of personal history. Enslaved persons were listed in the inventory of a will along with the bed, kitchenware, real estate and livestock, in each case assigned a value. Probate records are by far the most abundant documents that make it clear that, despite any protestations of humanity, enslaved persons were in the final analysis a man's property and part of his worth. Probate records depended on several circumstances to provide information. Not everyone had a will, but for those who did, many have now been scanned and are accessible online with searchable databases.[71] Other slaveowners died after the 1783 court ruling against enslavement and accordingly left no enslaved persons in their wills. For example, Colonel John Noyes, a known slaveowner during his lifetime, died in 1785 without any mention of enslaved persons.

While it has been noted that owners usually left one or, at most, two enslaved persons on their deaths, David Baldwin of Sudbury surpassed that figure when he died in 1770, only a year before the census of 1771.[72] In his will, he left six enslaved persons, one to each of his children—to son William

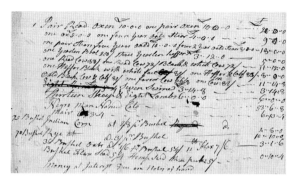

Left: At his death in 1775, Jonas Noyes listed one enslaved person, a "Negro man named Cato," in his probate inventory. *Copy of the original courtesy of the Wayland Historical Society.*

Below: Noyes-Morse House (also known as the Jonas Noyes House), still standing in Wayland, was the home of Cato, enslaved by Jonas Noyes. *Courtesy of the Wayland Historical Society.*

"a negro boy named Juba," and five "negro girls," Candace, Violet, Nancy, Cloe and Nell, one to each of his daughters. If there was any relationship between any of these "servants for life," it was totally ignored, as were any friendships that might have developed.

A "Negro man named Cato" is listed in the inventory of the will of Jonas Noyes, who died in 1775 from smallpox.[73] He was valued at £53.6.8, the same price that Jonas paid in 1767 when he purchased Cato from his father, Colonel John Noyes. Cato, as was true for most enslaved persons, was listed in the section devoted to the enumeration and value of livestock and farm produce, placed under sheep and lambs and above Indian corn.

Josiah Richardson Sr. left three enslaved persons on his death in 1770: his "negro girl" Dinah to his wife, Experience, and his "Negro" man Francis Benson to his son Josiah Jr. Dinah's son, Cesar, then seven years old, received special mention.[74] Cesar was given to Experience to be "at her own Disposell [*sic*]," stipulating that in the likelihood that Cesar outlived Experience, he would then go to son Josiah Jr. Young Cesar predeceased his new owner, dying at the age of eleven in 1773, leaving Dinah not only a widow but also childless.

Daniel Wyman left "freedom clothes" to Ashbel and Hagar, as listed in his probate inventory dated August 1766.[75] But since the recipients were not also included in the inventory, they were presumably freed prior to his death, although no records of their existence in Sudbury have been found to confirm this.

VITAL RECORDS[76]

Vital records for colonial Sudbury are hit or miss but can be useful when they exist. By far the most entries are for marriages rather than for births or deaths. These records also present one fairly unique problem: one must check both Sudbury's vital records and those of Wayland (Sudbury until 1780, East Sudbury until 1835 and thereafter Wayland) to get a clearer picture. For example, the marriage of Cuff and Hagar is recorded only in the Sudbury vital records, even though they lived on the east (modern Wayland) side. Cuff and Hagar were listed in a category titled "Negroes, Etc.," separated from other members of the Noyes family. All other marriages of persons of color were recorded alphabetically by name and without mention of race or whether they were enslaved, free or freed. One can only deduce their race and status through the existence of other documented sources. In 1761, when Francis Benson, still known to be enslaved by Josiah Richardson Sr., and Hannah Harry, freed by Reverend Loring, married, they were listed in the Sudbury vital records under their respective last names with no indication that they were non-white. A further complication can be found in misspellings and, in the case of some of the formerly enslaved, the adoption of a last or new name. The birth records of four children of Boston and Annah Paul were listed alphabetically along with white births in the Wayland vital records. After being freed, Boston and his family adopted the last name of his former master, Roby.

Vital records can often be supplemented by looking at church records.

Artist's rendering of the fourth meetinghouse/church on the east side of the Sudbury River, completed in 1726 after the town divided into two precincts. *Drawing by Rita Anderson, 1980.*

CHURCH RECORDS[77]

Existing church records identify a number of enslaved people and their owners who would otherwise remain unknown. These include records of births, baptisms, marriages and burials. Burial records were kept by the West Side (later Sudbury) Church's minister, Jacob Bigelow, from 1772 to 1816 and include the deaths of Frank Benson's first wife, Hannah, in 1774 and his second wife, Rose, in 1803. Baptisms were recorded in "Israel Loring's Book of Church Records," along with a list of church members and those who "owned the covenant." Owning the covenant was a prerequisite in the Congregational Church for receiving baptism, and the records confirm that for the enslaved, both rituals were performed on the same day. Church membership was a rare occurrence for African Americans in the colonial period, whether enslaved, free or freed, and in addition to Nero Benson, only two other named members are recorded for the West Side Church in colonial times.

PART III

THE REVOLUTIONARY WAR YEARS, 1775–1783

Chapter 8

PATRIOTS OF COLOR

An Overview

O n the first day of the American Revolution, April 19, 1775, almost 250 men from Sudbury answered the call to march to nearby Concord. Sudbury, the second-largest town in Middlesex County with a population of about 2,000, was a self-sufficient farming community made up of families that traced their ancestry to the British Isles. Many families were interrelated, and many were descended from the original Puritan settlers. There were 250 households, 464 swine, the same number of oxen and nearly double that number of milch cows and a small number of enslaved people. There was no wealthy or merchant class, but there were some prosperous farmers. All were concerned with the daily business of making a living from the land. Some of the men in town had seen service in the French and Indian War and were ready on April 19 to take up arms on behalf of their neighbors downriver in Concord.[78] Hundreds of Sudbury men would fight throughout the war. Of these, 6 have been identified as Patriots of color.

Massachusetts contributed the highest number of African and Indian Patriots throughout the war—more than any other colony. Two comprehensive online resources give information on the military records of men who fought in the American Revolution from Massachusetts: *Massachusetts Soldiers and Sailors in the American Revolution* (seventeen volumes) and National Society Daughters of the American Revolution's website *Forgotten Patriots: African American and American Indian Patriots in the Revolutionary War.* Together, these two sources identify the six Patriots of color, all privates, who enlisted from

Sudbury (including one from East Sudbury after the town divided in 1780): Porter Cuddy, Nicodemus Gigger (Gidger), Fortune Homer and Cuff Nimrod (Nimro, Nimroe, Nimroo) are listed in both the DAR listings and *Masachusetts Soldiers and Sailors*, while Jacob Speen and Samuel Ephraim are listed only in the latter. Additionally, Jacob Speen, Porter Cuddy and Cuff Nimrod appear in *Patriots of Color: 'A Peculiar Beauty and Merit,'* prepared by George Quintal Jr. for the National Park Service to commemorate Black and Indigenous soldiers who fought on the Battle Road on April 19, 1775, and at Bunker Hill in June of that year.

No more than a third of Blacks who bore arms were racially labeled, so other indicators were used to determine race, including names like Scipio, Cuff and Pompey or descriptive terms such as "dark complexion" or "wool hair." It should also be noted that muster rolls did not distinguish between enslaved and free. Except in very rare instances, units were integrated. These sources offer only records of military service with no insight into the lives of enlistees, including those of Sudbury, before or after their service. With the probable exception of Cuff Nimrod, they appear to have little or no connection to Sudbury in written records.

These enlistments from Sudbury do, however, highlight the historically close ties between the southeast corner of colonial Sudbury (now the Wayland section called Cochituate) and the adjacent Praying Indian town of Natick. With the exception of Porter Cuddy and Fortune Homer, all the others have known ties to Natick either through marriage or residency. While the ties to Natick are obvious in the Revolutionary War period, it is not known what earlier contacts may have occurred between the two towns.

Chapter 9

SUDBURY'S PATRIOTS OF COLOR

PORTER CUDDY

We know very little about Porter Cuddy, who enlisted from Sudbury on May 31, 1775, soon after the Battles of Lexington and Concord on April 19. His possible connections to Sudbury, other than his first enlistment, are unknown. Listed as "negro," he fought at the Battle of Bunker Hill, where he lost a coat. He later applied for reimbursement for the coat, and payment was eventually made to the captain of his company, Aaron Haynes of Sudbury. After the British evacuation of Boston on March 17, 1776, Cuddy reenlisted for a short second term in a Plymouth County regiment, which took him to the seaside town of Hull, Massachusetts. According to *Patriots of Color: 'A Peculiar Beauty and Merit'* by George Quintal, the possibility exists that Cuddy put out to sea "as a coastal observer." After that, Cuddy disappears from written records, and no further military service is recorded. Whether he was enslaved remains unknown, but certainly the possibility exists that Cuddy might have been seeking freedom.

FORTUNE HOMER

We know even less about Fortune Homer, who enlisted from Sudbury on a day not specified in *Massachusetts Soldiers and Sailors*. The first mention of his service is for the year 1777, when he enlisted in the Continental Army. Pay accounts for the Continental army list his service as running from April 12 to April 20, 1777, when it was reported that he had died. His connection to Sudbury remains unknown. While not identified by race, his first name, like Cuff Nimrod's, is a strong indication that he was once enslaved and perhaps still was, either in Sudbury or elsewhere. He was also the only person of color from Sudbury who reportedly died in the Revolutionary War.

Cuff Nimrod

Cuff Nimrod has a longer documented history in Sudbury than any other veteran of color. Whereas the other soldiers from Sudbury had names more associated with Indigenous people or free Blacks, Cuff Nimrod's first and last names are indicative of a person who had been, or perhaps remained, enslaved. Although not identified by race in his military records, the name "Cuff" is often associated with African American slavery.[79] His last name went through a number of spellings, from Nimroo to Nemro and finally Nimrod, making it reasonable to assume that he had adopted a last name rather than acquired it at birth.

Cuff Nimrod, estimated to be in his early twenties, enlisted from Sudbury on April 30, 1775, and served during the Battle of Bunker Hill and the Siege of Boston. His last date of service was in 1776, while still residing in Sudbury. He was living in Sudbury at the time of his marriage in Natick to Olive Kent on January 14, 1779.[80] His short service and longer stay in Sudbury open up the possibility that, enslaved or freed, he had responsibilities toward someone (possibly an enslaver) in town. While he is known to have spent at least four years as a Sudbury resident, the details of his time in town have not yet emerged.

Jacob Speen

There is no evidence that Jacob Speen ever lived in Sudbury. He almost certainly descended from a founding family of Natick Praying Indians, originally established by the Reverend John Eliot in 1651 to Christianize Native Americans. Listed as a "Negro" in his service record, Jacob Speen certainly was of Indigenous ancestry, while it is unknown whether he also had African ancestors. Intermarriages were common between persons of color, while not permitted with white people under the laws of Massachusetts.

Several of the Sudbury veterans married women from Natick, only one of whom can be documented as Indigenous. Several were known to live there when their service ended. Speen married Dinah Pero of Cambridge in Natick in February 1776[81] but continued to serve.

Speen enlisted from Sudbury on April 27, 1775, at the age of twenty, shortly after the Battles of Lexington and Concord, and fought at the Battle of Bunker Hill. He served throughout the war in the Massachusetts Militia, enlisting for service in Cambridge the second time. He continued to reenlist at various times for particular tours of duty, for which he collected bounties for service. His primary service was from Natick, where he is known to have resided by 1781. According to George Quintal, in 1782 Speen accepted a bounty to serve in the Continental army. In addition to responding to the spirit of independence and adventure, it was not uncommon for young men to enlist for short periods and reenlist as a means of earning multiple bounties for their service and, in Speen's case, providing for a wife.

It is possible that at the time of his first enlistment, Jacob Speen was working in Sudbury as a hired hand during planting season, but there is no evidence of a longer association with the town. There is no indication that he was ever enslaved.

NICODEMUS GIGGER

In contrast to the scarcity of information on the other Patriots of Color who enlisted from Sudbury, there is ample documentation for Nicodemus Gigger under multiple variations of the spelling of his name. In 2012, the Massachusetts Society of Genealogists magazine featured an article tracing Nicodemus Gigger and his family.[82] The first mention of Sudbury occurred on February 26, 1764, when Nicodemus and Jane Nimery of Sudbury were married in Lynn, Massachusetts. They were both listed as "Negroes," although Jane might have had mixed ancestry with ties to the Praying Indian town of Natick. In 1767, they had a child in Natick, and Nicodemus was also in Natick when he married for the second time (presumably after Jane's death), this time to a woman from Medway in 1773. The second mention of Sudbury in the magazine article is Nicodemus Gigger's enlistment on October 7, 1775, as a private in Colonel William Prescott's regiment. No other service is recorded. Nicodemus was definitely living in Natick in 1777, when he married his third wife, Beulah Speen Rogers, an Indigenous woman. A native of Natick, Beulah had spent time in the North End of

Boston, where she had married Saul Rogers, an enslaved Black man, at the Old North Church in 1767. Nicodemus and Beulah Gigger spent the rest of their lives in Natick. They died four months apart in 1802. There is no evidence that Nicodemus Gigger was ever enslaved, but he illustrates the lack of opportunity for a free Black man who had to move from town to town to find work. Although he was finally accepted as a resident of Natick, he had been warned out of other towns in his younger days.

Samuel Ephraim

Samuel Ephraim is another example of the close association between Sudbury and Natick. An Indigenous man born in Natick, he enlisted for the newly formed town of East Sudbury on December 2, 1780. Ephraim, seventeen, listed as a farmer, answered the call for volunteers from Middlesex County soon after he was eligible for service. By this stage of the war, recruits were hard to come by. Many towns could not fulfill their quotas, and Samuel Ephraim, a resident of Natick, agreed to "serve to the credit of the Town of East Sudbury."[83] No other associations with Sudbury or East Sudbury are known.

From these few examples, it is obvious that the nearness of Natick to Sudbury was of mutual benefit. Both Praying Indians and African Americans, many enslaved, had a very small pool of people with whom to form social ties or find mates. People of color could interact more freely with each other than with those who were white, as intimacy between Blacks and whites was proscribed by law.

Intermarriage between Indigenous women and African American men was a way to widen the choices. As enslavement followed the mother's status, marriages between enslaved men and free Indigenous women ensured that any children they had would be born free.[84]

Chapter 10

TOWARD INDEPENDENCE

The outbreak of the Revolutionary War accelerated a shift in attitudes that was already becoming evident as early as the Lost Census of 1765, which noted that "the People here are very much tired of Negro Servants." According to Jared Ross Hardesty, "Before the 1760s, there was little criticism of slavery in the North as an institution. Regardless of its brutality and inhumanity, slavery was ultimately a pragmatic, commonplace solution to labor shortages."[85] Numerous resources, including Professor David Hackett Fischer's *Paul Revere's Ride*, detail the period between the end of the last French and Indian War in 1763 and the start of the Revolution in 1775. These years were marked by increasing pressure from Great Britain to assert authority over the American colonies and curtail the liberties of the British citizenry in North America. New forms of taxation to replenish the coffers of the British treasury depleted by the French and Indian Wars and its aftermath, such as the Stamp Act in 1765, became a source of extreme outrage in the colonies. This was especially true in Massachusetts, whose political leaders and citizenry took great pride in their right to govern themselves, a tradition that went back to the earliest settlements.[86] Resistance to increasing pressure by the British government to force the American colonies to comply with this new way of extracting taxes culminated in the Boston Tea Party in December 1773, which led to the imposition of what amounted to martial law in Massachusetts by the British government. The more resistance, the more severe the punishments for those who long considered themselves proud

Englishmen with the right to govern themselves and to raise revenue to see to their local needs within the sprawling British empire. A spirit of defiance was in the air in Massachusetts by 1775, embraced by political figures, ministers and patriotic citizens. Talk of liberty and freedom rang out to stir the passions and prepare the citizenry for the struggles ahead. Patriotic ministers exhorted their male townsmen in fiery speeches to join the militia to combat British tyranny and assume their fundamental rights as Englishmen. Among them was Reverend William Emerson of Concord, the owner of the aforementioned Frank Benson and several other enslaved persons. According to Reverend Emerson's grandson Ralph Waldo Emerson in his 1835 "Historical Discourse" in Concord, "The cause of the colonies was so much in his heart, that he did not cease to make it the subject of his preaching and his prayers, and is said to have deeply inspired many of his people with his own enthusiasm." Surely, Reverend Emerson's words had an impact not only on the free citizens of Concord but also on those who were in bondage.

While restrictions to freedom were a part of daily life for Blacks and Indigenous people, such as Reverend Emerson's enslaved man Frank, they were unfamiliar infringements on the authority of many political figures, merchants and clergymen—in other words, white men. In "African Slavery in America," Thomas Paine made this clear in a newspaper in March 1775, shortly before war broke out in Massachusetts:

> *With what consistency, or decency* [Americans] *complain so loudly of attempts to enslave them, while they hold so many hundred thousands in slavery; and annually enslave many thousands more, without any pretense of authority, or claim upon them?*

Massachusetts may have progressed further than any other colony in eradicating slavery, but at the start of the American Revolution, it had not yet ended. The turmoil of the Revolutionary War, with its rallying cries of natural rights, equality, independence and liberty, provided more opportunities for enslaved and marginalized Blacks to bring to fruition long-cherished dreams of freedom.

Black people, especially the enslaved, embraced the chance to gain freedom through enlisting. They had little to lose. According to historian John Hannigan, who researched and wrote a number of scholarly articles on soldiers of color for Minute Man National Historical Park in 2014:

> *At no time during the American Revolution did the Continental Congress or the Massachusetts government offer freedom to slaves in exchange for their enlistment in the military. This means that any negotiation on this subject took place between individual slaves and their owners, recruiting officers and men of color, or drafted men and black substitutes.*[87]

Freedom for service became increasingly obtainable for a number of reasons between owners and the enslaved. Slaves received bounties for enlisting, which could be used as part of a settlement for their freedom. Owners wanted slaves for their labor, and if they were in the service, they were of little benefit to them. Some slaves bypassed any formalities, enlisted and simply ran away from their masters, never to return. Most men of color lived marginalized lives, and enlistment bounties were a beacon of hope to try to improve their economic condition, whether enslaved or free. Severe manpower shortages to win the war contributed to a need for able-bodied soldiers and sailors, and Black men and other persons of color seized on every opportunity to escape, even if it meant risking their lives, as is evidenced by Sudbury enlistees.

DINAH

The Revolutionary War changed not only the lives of enslaved or marginalized Black men but also the lives of enslaved or marginalized Black women. As of this writing, Dinah is the only woman whose documented life encompasses the journey from enslavement in Sudbury to freedom after the Revolution.

Soon after the signing of the Declaration of Independence, Experience Wight Richardson, the widow of Josiah Richardson Sr., who had lived with enslaved persons for most of her life, freed her enslaved woman, Dinah. On December 9, 1776, Richardson recorded: "This day my servant Dinah had her freedom."

Less than a month after freeing her, on January 2, 1777, Experience Richardson made another entry into her diary: "O that now I live alone I may converse with God more than ever, the last of my famaly [*sic*] is gone now that Dinah is gone."

Unlike many others who were freed from bondage with few options as to places to go and so stayed with their former masters, Dinah did not remain in the Richardson house. As recounted in an earlier chapter, Dinah, a widow

Known today as the Israel Howe Brown House in Sudbury, this was earlier the home of Josiah Richardson Sr. and at least three enslaved persons: Francis Benson, Dinah and her son Cesar. *Photo by Rachael Robinson.*

who had lost a husband and child during her time with the Richardsons, persevered. Wherever she lived before 1781 when she remarried, it was presumably not with Experience Richardson. When Dinah married Cuff Kneeland of Lincoln on February 8, 1781, the marriage was recorded as taking place in East Sudbury, although she gave her place of residence as Sudbury. According to Richard C. Wiggin in *Embattled Farmers*, which documents Revolutionary War veterans in neighboring Lincoln, Cuff Kneeland had also obtained his freedom in 1776 and had previously been enslaved by John Hoar of Lincoln. Known while enslaved as Cuff Hoar, he changed his name to Kneeland in 1780. The vital record of their marriage refers to Dinah as Dinah Young. The possibility of it not being the Dinah enslaved by the Richardson family is unlikely due to several factors. Her choice of last name reflects the spirit of someone who may have been quite young when she was first married and had a child and an affirmation that she still had a life ahead of her. Her choice of mate was from Lincoln, as was her first husband, an area she might have been familiar with. Lastly, no other Dinah has been recorded as living in Sudbury at that time. Of course, it would have been ideal if Experience Wight Richardson had mentioned this second marriage in her diary. She lived until 1786, but by 1781, her diary entries are quite limited and ended in 1782.

Cuff Kneeland died a month after their wedding, leaving Dinah widowed yet again. On January 22, 1783, Dinah Kneelie (a corruption of Kneeland) was married for the third time in Sudbury to Cato Walker, a freed slave from Worcester.[88] According to the *History of Worcester, Massachusetts* by William Lincoln, Dinah moved to Worcester, where Cato Walker received a small business loan from Worcester Town Meeting to help set up as a blacksmith. He was on the tax rolls by 1785, and by the late 1780s, he was one of five African American heads of household. Dinah predeceased her husband in Worcester in 1807, hopefully having enjoyed more contentment than she had found in Sudbury.

PART IV

THE LEGACY OF SLAVERY

Chapter 11

THE SLOW DEATH OF SLAVERY

IN SUDBURY

As was true for the rest of Massachusetts, slavery in Sudbury didn't
end so much as fade away.[89] And like so much regarding the lives of
enslaved people, the end of slavery in colonial Sudbury is shrouded
in mystery. Who were the last enslaved persons in town? When did they
become free? And how? All unknown. Again, the first federal census in 1790
listed no enslaved persons in Massachusetts. In 1780, the constitution of
the newly formed Commonwealth of Massachusetts, the first in the nation
and a model for the United States Constitution, declared, "All men are
born free and equal, and have…the right of enjoying and defending their
lives and liberty." Freedom suits followed in which the enslaved sued their
owners for freedom. The Supreme Judicial Court of Massachusetts held
that laws and customs that sanctioned slavery were incompatible with the
new state constitution. Many researchers of colonial slavery agree that these
court cases, which denied the individual owners the right to hold human
property, was the death knell but not the definitive end of enslavement in
Massachusetts. Since no law was passed by the Commonwealth stipulating
a precise date, it is likely that slavery lingered on past 1783. In The Wayside
Inn Archives, there is a receipt for payment for a "Negro garll" [*sic*] that
Ezekiel Howe of Sudbury purchased for £200 in Boston on December 10,
1779, three years after the Declaration of Independence was signed.[90] That
is the last known documentation of an enslaved person in Sudbury. Anything
past that date has not yet surfaced.

Colonel Ezekiel How buys a "negro garll" for £200 in 1779 during the American Revolution. This is the last documented purchase of an enslaved person in colonial Sudbury. *Original in The Wayside Inn Archives and Research Center, Sudbury.*

THE ROBY FAMILY

Enslavement could cast a long shadow. As late as 1824, according to records from the Wayland town clerk's office, the overseers of the poor of Boston wrote to the overseers of the poor of East Sudbury asking to be reimbursed for the care of Mary Sinnes, whose mother, Venus, was the daughter of Boston Roby, once enslaved by Dr. Ebenezer Roby. Dr. Roby, who studied at Harvard and abroad, was one of the most prominent men in town and much in demand. In addition to serving patients in colonial Sudbury, he cared for many in neighboring towns. His account books include treatment for a number of African Americans and Indigenous people. Housed at Harvard's Countway Library, his accounts detail his medical career and provide insights into the ailments of his day. In 1772, when Dr. Roby died, he left the enslaved Boston to his son, Ebenezer Jr. He also stipulated that Boston should help his daughter take care of her garden, cut her wood and help her in any way that he could. Clearly, Boston—referred to in the Wayland Vital Records and East Sudbury Church Records as Boston Paul—remained enslaved. But was the rest of the family also enslaved? Boston and Annah Paul had four children whose births are recorded: Sippio in 1767, the aforementioned Venus in 1773, Cesar in 1775 and son and namesake Boston in 1781. Although Sippio was born before Dr. Roby's death in 1772, only Boston, the father and husband, was mentioned in his will, suggesting that Annah and young Sippio were not enslaved. Nevertheless, the overseers of the poor in East Sudbury in 1824 had no problem believing that the whole family had been enslaved by the Robys. According to their reply to the Boston overseers, they "doubted not that

Old Roby House was the first home of Nero Benson in colonial Sudbury and later was home to Boston Paul, enslaved by Dr. Ebenezer Roby. The house was destroyed by fire in 1887. *Courtesy of Historic New England.*

Mary [Sinnes's] mother Venus and her grandparents, Boston and Annah, were slaves." But in no case was East Sudbury liable for Mary's care, as they made clear in their answer to the Boston overseers, which cited an 1819 Massachusetts Supreme Judicial Court case:

> *In the case of the* Inhabitants of Lanesborough vs. the Inhabitants of Westfield,…*which is a case precisely to the point, it was decided that the children of slaves under the provincial government were not slaves & derived no settlement from either parents or parents' masters, but were* <u>*Children of the Commonwealth.*</u> *Having, therefore, so high an Authority to rely upon, we object to paying the expense now arising in your alms house on account of this woman, as we deny her settlement's being here.*[91]

Well into the first quarter of the nineteenth century, it was important for local officials to keep up with judicial determinations of cases dealing with enslavement to ensure that their towns would not incur any expense for the descendants of those who had been enslaved in their communities. The legacy of enslavement in Massachusetts wove a tangled web even for those who were not alive to experience it firsthand.

Chapter 12

THE MEANING OF FREEDOM

After slavery ended in Massachusetts and some northern states, what remained was the sentiment expressed at the beginning of this book with the words of Lydia Maria Child in 1833: "The form of slavery does not exist among us; but the very spirit of the hateful and mischievous thing is here in all its strength." According to historian Lorenzo Greene, "Legally, the freedmen held an intermediate status somewhat higher than that of slaves, but palpably lower than that of free white persons."[92] Freedom brought few or no opportunities for the vast majority of emancipated Black people. As they received no pay for their years of toil for others, there was no money with which those who had been enslaved could, in all but a few rare instances, acquire land of their own or set up a household. Many are known to have remained with their former enslavers, as they most likely could not afford to live anywhere else. Perhaps a few who had skills learned from their owners could find some employment, but most of the enslaved in Sudbury worked as farmhands or domestic servants. Some of those who had been freed before, during or after the Revolutionary War moved to urban areas where there were more opportunities for adults and children. Men could work as laborers and women as domestics, and children could find work in the homes of white families. Boston Roby and his family left East Sudbury after he gained his freedom and are listed in the 1790 federal census in Boston; Dinah moved to Worcester, where her husband found work as a blacksmith.

In the first federal census in 1790, eleven persons of color in East Sudbury (Wayland) and Sudbury were living in households headed by a man who was white: two in Sudbury and nine in East Sudbury. Several of the men, including William Baldwin in East Sudbury and Ezekiel Howe in Sudbury, had been known slaveowners. By 1800, three Blacks are listed as living in East Sudbury and none in Sudbury. According to Professor Ira Berlin in his groundbreaking book on the first two centuries of slavery in America, *Many Thousands Gone*, "By the third decade of the nineteenth century, black northerners had almost entirely abandoned the countryside." Those who remained "took their place among the North's landless farmhands (almost exclusively males) who annually contracted with farmers in exchange for the right to a cottage, a garden, a woodlot, and occasionally a token sum of money." For widows and women like Rose Benson, freedom was even more of a struggle, with domestic work their only option.

PETER BOOZ AND FLORA AND THOSE WHO STAYED

When Colonel John Noyes died in 1785, he left no enslaved persons, although the genealogy of his family proclaimed that he had owned "a considerable number of slaves." Two graves in Wayland's North Cemetery have long been identified as enslaved persons belonging to Colonel John Noyes, whose large tombstone is nearby. The small markers for Peter Booz and Flora stand out from any others in that section, as they are placed at right angles to all the other stones, which face east. Since they lived into the first quarter of the nineteenth century, neither Peter Booz nor Flora was enslaved when they died. But were they in fact enslaved by Colonel Noyes? For Flora, as is true for many enslaved women, there is no documentation, although it is likely she was once enslaved, as it does not appear that she ever had a last name. The record is clearer for Peter Booz, as adult free men, but not women, were assessed a poll tax.[93]

Assessor's records for East Sudbury list the names of those who paid a poll tax, as well as taxes for real estate and personal property.[94] At this time, the poll tax, or head tax, was a flat rate for each individual male irrespective of any other assets he might have. In 1785, 1786 and 1787, a Black man with the name Peter Noyes was assessed for a poll tax. In 1788, there was no poll tax assessed to Peter Noyes, but there was one for Peter Booz, hinting at a change of name. Since Peter Booz is buried near Colonel Noyes's grave and the story that came down through Wayland history says he was once enslaved by Colonel Noyes, this increases its likelihood. Since women did not pay a poll tax, there is no mention of Flora or any other Black female in the assessor's records, nor is there any indication that any Black women owned real estate or personal property. A "Black woman" named Flora is listed in the East Sudbury death records for 1823. Presumably this is the Flora who is buried near Peter Booz and Colonel John Noyes in Wayland's North Cemetery.

As a free male, Peter Booz continued to be assessed a poll tax every year through 1815, after which his name disappears from the assessor's records. He was not taxed for real estate or personal estate during those years except for 1809 and 1810, when he was assessed a poll tax and a very small personal estate, but no real estate. The personal estate tax indicates that Peter Booz probably acquired something of

The graves of Peter Booz and Flora in Wayland's North Cemetery are at right angles to their likely enslaver, Colonel John Noyes. *Author's collection.*

value during those years, which disappeared from the tax rolls after that.

Beyond the gravestones of Peter Booz and Flora in Wayland's North Cemetery, there is little information on what life was like for those who stayed. From Ezekiel Howe's will, we learn that Portsmouth also remained in rural Sudbury until his death in 1799, serving his former master at Howe's Tavern (The Wayside Inn) in some capacity, as specified earlier in the codicil to Howe's will. Jube Freenow was also assessed a poll tax into the early 1800s and was likely once enslaved by William Baldwin after Baldwin's father, David, died and left "Juba" to his son in his will. Perhaps Jube celebrated his freedom with the newly adopted last name of Freenow, but he appears to have continued to live with the Baldwin family even after his former master's death. Several other names of Black men appear sporadically on the tax records as owing a poll tax, but they disappear within a year or two. They may have come to do farm work and only stayed a short time. In the early 1800s, as was true in 1790, no Black men were listed as heads of household, and none owned property. They continued to work for white families if indeed they found any work at all.

CONCLUSION

Certainly, there is evidence that some degree of antislavery sentiment existed in colonial Massachusetts. As early as 1700, Judge Samuel Sewall published *The Selling of Joseph*, the first antislavery tract published in New England, but in general, arguments against enslavement were few and far between. They became more prevalent as the events leading to the start of the American Revolution unfolded with increasing cries from white townspeople that they were being treated like slaves by the British government. Being treated as slaves was a reality for enslaved Black people who were abolitionists long before any white persons promoted such sentiments. Many seized upon the revolutionary rhetoric to actively pursue their long-cherished dreams of freedom.

It is impossible to assess the degree of antislavery sentiment that prevailed in colonial Sudbury, if indeed any existed, or whether and how it might have evolved over the years. Did Arabella Read change her mind about enslavement when she died in 1717 and freed Frank? She certainly had ample opportunity to do so during the years that she owned her. What motivated Samuel Wood to emancipate Nero Benson in 1747 at considerable expense to himself? What traits or characteristics found in Nero Benson led to this decision? The freedom of Nero Benson is the only documented emancipation paper for an enslaved person living in Sudbury. Did any men of means in Sudbury resist the opportunity to acquire enslaved labor because they had similar views to John Adams, who refused to own any? No documented evidence of antislavery sentiment or objections to bondage in Sudbury during the period in which it was practiced has surfaced as of this writing. To repeat the words of Professor Jared Ross Hardesty, "Before the 1760s, there was little criticism of slavery in the North as an institution. Regardless of its brutality and inhumanity, slavery was ultimately a pragmatic, commonplace solution to labor shortages."[95]

That would not be the case as we move into the nineteenth century. By the 1830s, there were antislavery societies operating in both Sudbury and East Sudbury (Wayland after 1835). They joined with a number of people, largely women, in the Northeast to oppose slavery and some forms of segregation. They submitted numerous petitions to Congress to protest the existence of slavery throughout the South and in the nation's capital, where the institution was flourishing. The abolitionist movement was still in its infancy, but a few brave women and men stepped up to protest what they considered a blemish on this country. Turning their attention outward, rarely did anyone refer to New England's slave past and the legacy it left on the region.

A document housed in the Goodnow Library's local history collection offers a glimmer of light on the subject. Dr. Thomas Stearns, a physician and Sudbury resident, started collecting bits and pieces of local history in the 1830s, including a bill of sale for Frank Benson dating to 1745. On the back of the bill of sale, Dr. Stearns added a personal notation about the seller and the sold:

> *Rev. John Swift was minister of Acton. The Negro mentioned in the foregoing pages was a very honest fellow. Either he or his son was a member of the church and died in good in the faith and left behind him a fair reputation.*[96] *How any man professing to be a minister of Christ could be guilty of the atrocious crime of trafficking in human flesh is inconceivable to us at the present day. Or how that anyone could be blind to the strange inconsistency of owning his fellow, as a brother at the Lord's table, and in all other places treat him as a brute. Whatever the errors of the times may be, let me ever rejoice that the sin of slavery is no longer tolerated in this land of boasted liberty.*[97]

Dr. Stearns's comments can be read in various ways. His assessment of Frank's character points out his human qualities and not his enslavement. His strong condemnation of Reverend John Swift of Acton, Massachusetts, and other ministers who owned enslaved persons emphasizes both the hypocrisy and brutality of slaveowning. These are strong antislavery statements regarding a shameful part of America's history. Yet when Dr. Stearns died in 1844, the "sin of slavery" was not gone from America. It was an established institution that would divide the nation and lead to the Civil War less than twenty years after his death. The "land of liberty" that had rid itself of this evil is certainly not America but Sudbury and parts of the North. Ministers in the South continued to own slaves. And what about

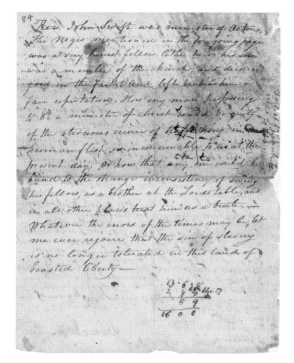

Dr. Thomas Stearns, a physician who collected old documents on Sudbury's history, wrote his thoughts on colonial enslavement on the back of Frank Benson's bill of sale. *Courtesy of the Goodnow Library.*

Sudbury? What was Stearns referring to when he wrote about the land of "boasted liberty"? What exactly was he rejoicing over?

Many historians contend that slavery in Massachusetts was more humane than slavery in the southern colonies. Most Massachusetts enslaved persons did not live substantially different lives from those of their white masters with regard to their daily activities. Slaves and masters often worked together, lived together, went to the same churches and shared many hardships. However, no enslaved person could live with a family of his choosing or have the freedom to make his own decisions. Few in number, they were isolated from a natural need to associate with others who shared similar circumstances. In addition, being recognized as a person but classified as an animal or piece of furniture for tax purposes or in probate records can only be construed as enforcing and perpetuating fundamental inequality. To watch a child being sold away, or to be sold away and your child left behind or be denied the right to live with a spouse, is dehumanizing. Slavery was an atrocity, whether in the South or the North—a life not of one's own making but controlled by others.

The legacy of slavery is still with us in continued racial divisiveness and strife; its deep roots in the past have impacted our lives today. Enslavement died, but the prejudices against Black people remained. The Puritan Village had an underside that also helped to define it. There is still more to do.

Appendix

TIMELINE OF ENSLAVEMENT

IN COLONIAL SUDBURY

SA = Sudbury Archives

Date/Year	Type of Reference (Event)	Name of the Enslaved	Name of Slaveowner (if applicable)
1638	European settlement of Sudbury	N/A	N/A
26 Feb. 1638	Slaves from West Indies to MA	N/A	N/A
1641	MA is first colony to legalize slavery	N/A	N/A
1644	Enslaved from Africa to MA	N/A	N/A
9 Jan. 1654	Town Meeting—Divisions of the land	N/A	N/A

Source	Notes
Powell, *Puritan Village*	As of 1780, Sudbury Plantation (later colonial Sudbury) separated into two towns, Sudbury and East Sudbury. In 1835, East Sudbury was renamed Wayland.
Gov. John Winthrop https:// archive.org, 254. Original at Massachusetts Historical Society	Many historians use Winthrop's entry on this date as the first known mention of slaves from the West Indies.
Moore, *Notes on the History of Slavery in Massachusetts*, 11	"The Body of Liberties" Massachusetts Bay Colony Law.
Greene, *Negro in Colonial New England*, 20	"...an association of business men sent three ships there for gold dust and Negroes."
SA #284 Original Town Clerk's Office, Town Records, Book I	Raises possibility of enslaved persons in colonial Sudbury. "The lands shall be divided by the inhabitants according to their several estates and families and counting the family to be the husband, wife, children and such servants as men have that they have either *bought* or brought up."

APPENDIX

Date/Year	Type of Reference (Event)	Name of the Enslaved	Name of Slaveowner (if applicable)
1661	Probate	N/A	N/A
1665/6	Middlesex County Court Records	Negro boy	Benjamin Crane
1670	Middlesex County Court Records	Katharina	Joseph Deakin (not Sudbury resident)
1674/5	Death	Elizabeth	Joseph Noyes
1697	Probate	Sambo	Thomas Walker
1698	Land purchase in Westboro	Nanny	Peter Goulding
1701	Probate Record	"Frank" (female)	Thomas Read

Source	Notes
Abstract of will of Joseph Noyes dated 1659, SA #2643 Original in Sudbury Town Clerk's Office	No mention of slaves but left "what I have" in Barbados, a major center for the slave trade, to family members. He reportedly died in Barbados.
Middlesex County Court Folio Collection, Microfilm Reel 901008, Folio 233 (9). Accessed through MA Archives	Court Record: "Witnesses described the boy wearing a geer [*sic*] of wire, presumably a kind of muzzle, and a chain hobbling his feet. He had been heard screaming, 'O Lord! O Lord!' from a distance of a quarter of a mile off and he had 'many stripe wounds, some raw, some healed or partly healed.'" Quoted in *Sex in Middlesex*, 159
Middlesex County, MA: Abstracts of Court Records, 1643–1674, americanancestors.org Call #MSS 596	Peter Goulding was acting as attorney to Joseph Deakin against Thomas Jenner, Mariner, for "Negro called Katharina." Goulding later lived in colonial Sudbury and was a slaveowner.
New England Historical & Genealogical Register 17 (1863): 313	"Negro of Mr. Joseph Noyes," a member of the Noyes family originally from Newbury, MA. His genealogy states "he was a man of considerable property owning a considerable number of slaves."
Middlesex County, MA Probate File Papers: Vol. 2200–23,999, p. 23632	Sambo was bequeathed to his widow, Mary Walker. She married John Goodnow of Sudbury in 1705.
Forbes, *Hundredth Town*, 169 archive.org	"This farm [in Westboro] was afterwards sold to Peter Goulding, of Sudbury, 'for one negro wench called Nanny, delivered at £25.10, and £10. in money.'" This almost certainly was Sampson's mother (see 1703 and 1705/8 entries).
Will of Thomas Read of Sudbury; MA. Archives AA, Middlesex County, MA Probate File Papers, Vol. 1800–1999, p. 18620.1.	Bequeathed "Frank" to his wife, Arabella.

Date/Year	Type of Reference (Event)	Name of the Enslaved	Name of Slaveowner (if applicable)
1703	Probate Record	Sampson	Peter Goulding
1704/8	Middlesex County Court Records	Sampson	Alleged owners William Jennison and/or Thomas Brown
9 Mar. 1714	Birth	Simeon Harry, son of Henry and Frances Harry	N/A
26 Aug. 1716	Birth	Peter Harry, son of Henry and Frances Harry	N/A
1717	Probate of Arabella Read of Sudbury	"Frank" (female)	Arabella Read
1718	Probate Inventory	A "bought sarvant [sic] Maid"	Isaac Hunt
1719	Promise of freedom	Sambo	Mary Goodnow
1720	Probate	"Violate" (Violet)	Rev. Samuel Parris

Source	Notes
Will of Peter Goulding American Ancestors database, Middlesex County File Papers, Vol. Middlesex Cases 8000–9999, p. 9586.1.	In his probate inventory he listed "a negro sarvant boy" [sic] worth £20.
Record of William Jennison and Thomas Brown court cases in Family Search Folio 233, Group III—Middlesex County Probate Records Accessed through MA Archives	On Dec. 25, 1704, Jennison sold Sampson to Brown(e) for £30, claiming he had clear title to the boy. At this time, Sampson was still owned by the estate of Peter Goulding, Jennison's father-in-law. Jennison sued Brown for breach of contract. Both men lived in Sudbury.
Sudbury Vital Records	Race not specified until later entries. Unknown if any of them were enslaved or free at this time.
Sudbury Vital Records	Race not specified until later entries. Unknown if they were enslaved or free.
Middlesex County Probate Records, MA Archives, #18456 (microfilm in person) Also on americanancestors.org	Read granted freedom to Frank, made her sole executrix and heir. Frank was left to Arabella Read in the will of her husband, Thomas Read (see 1701 entry). Will dated 1716.
Americanancestors.org (Middlesex Cty. Probate Rec) Vol. 12000–13999, p. 12243	Valued at £8.
Mass. Land Records 1620–1986 Middlesex Deeds 1718–1722 vol. 20. Accessed on familysearch.org	Sambo was bequeathed to Mary Goodnow by her late husband, Thomas Walker, when he died in 1697.
Middlesex County Probate Records, MA Archives, #16951 (microfilm in person) Also on AA	Violet was left to his son and namesake, Samuel Parris.

Date/Year	Type of Reference (Event)	Name of the Enslaved	Name of Slaveowner (if applicable)
1721	Marriage	Nero Benson to Dido Dingo	Rev. John Swift
Pre-1725		Mention of possible enslaved persons Jack, Rose and Plato	Hopestill Bent
13 Mar. 1729	Accident	Negro servant	Josiah Brown
14 Dec. 1729	Death	Dinah	Hopestill Brown
3 Jan. 1730	Death	Negro (presumably male)	Abraham Briant
1730	Medical treatment	Francis Negro	Unknown
1731	Medical treatment	Grace, maid to Dr. Ebenezer Roby	Unknown
1733	Sale of enslaved person	Gloster	Jonathan Smith
Ca. 1734	Birth	Simeon	Rev. Israel Loring
1 Sept. 1734	Persons Who Accepted the Church Covenant 1723–1816 (west side)	Zilpah	Benjamin Wight of Sudbury

Source	Notes
Framingham Vital Records	Dido and Nero are listed separately as marrying each other: Benson, p. 239 Dingo, p. 268 and cited as "Negroes"
Natick Bulletin, May 22, 1925 Digitized by Morse Institute (Natick Public Library). Article was about the Jonathan Bacon House in Natick.	Has not been verified. Hopestill Bent left no enslaved persons when he died in Sudbury in 1725.
Journal of Rev. Israel Loring SA #13730 (transcription)	Enslaved man of Josiah Brown shot himself with a gun. Loring thought it was intentional.
Journal of Rev Israel Loring SA #12188 (transcription)	Hopestill Brown died the day before Dinah.
Journal of Rev Israel Loring SA #12189 (transcription)	
"Account Book of Dr. Ebenezer Roby 1730–31" On archive.org	Merely lists Francis as at Mr. Baldwin's without specifying what relationship they might have or whether Francis was enslaved, free or freed or male or female.
"Account Book of Dr. Ebenezer Roby 1730–31" On archive.org, hard copies at Wayland Museum and Historical Soc. and Wayland Lib.	Enslaved possibly; race not specified. Also medical treatment for Grace's Mother and Sister in March.
Hudson, *History of Sudbury* (SERVANTS pp. 143–144)	
Journal of Rev. Israel Loring SA #12197.	Recorded in Loring's *Journals* in 1755 at the time of Simeon's death. Simeon was 21 when he died, which puts his birthdate at 1733/34.
SA #15105 Original in Sudbury Town Clerk's Office, Church Records.	Also recorded as baptized the same day.

Date/Year	Type of Reference (Event)	Name of the Enslaved	Name of Slaveowner (if applicable)
9 Feb. 1735	List of Members of West Side Church	Zilpah	Benjamin Wight
12 Apr. 1736	Town Meeting	Mr. Baldwin's Negro	Mr. Baldwin
Dec. 1739	Illness	Hannah	Rev. Israel Loring
31 Aug. 1740	Illness	Simeon	Rev. Israel Loring
20 Jun. 1741	Seeking baptism	Simeon Harry	Unknown
28 Jun. 1741	Persons Who Accepted the Church Covenant 1723–1816 (west side)	Simeon Harry, Negro	Unknown
14 Jul. 1741	Seeking baptism	Peter Harry	Unknown
9 Aug. 1741	Persons Who Accepted the Church Covenant 1723–1816 (west side)	Sampson, Negro	Likely enslaved
Feb. 1742	Fire at the Loring Parsonage	Hannah	Rev. Israel Loring

Source	Notes
SA #15101. Original in Sudbury Town Clerk's Office, Church Records.	She had owned the covenant and been baptized the previous year.
SA #1526 (transcription) Handwritten copy in Town Clerk's Office, Sudbury, Book III.	Payment to "Mr. Baldwin's Negro for 28 Birds' heads." Most likely David Baldwin.
Journal of Rev. Israel Loring SA #12191 (transcription)	"Daughters Elizabeth and Sarah and maid servant [a euphemism for enslaved] Hannah are recovering from the measles."
Journal of Rev. Israel Loring (transcription) original at Goodnow Library	"I found Simeon considerably ill of the throat distemper....Hope it will please the Lord to deal with him." Not Simeon Harry, but young Simeon.
Journal of Rev. Israel Loring, Nov. 7, 1740–Apr. 25, 1742 SA #12192 (transcription)	"Simeon Harry a Negro was with me to desire baptism for himself. A person of Good knowledge declaring that he has been under awakenings by my late preaching." Simeon Harry lived in Framingham, and his status (enslaved, free or freed) is unknown. He is most likely the same Simeon who was born in Sudbury in 1714.
SA #15105 Original in Sudbury Town Clerk's Office in Church Records	He was also baptized that same day.
Journal of Rev. Israel Loring Nov. 7, 1740–Apr. 25, 1742 SA #12192 (transcription)	"Peter Harry was with me to Seek Baptism for himself. I examined him as to his knowledge in part and ordered him to Come again to me." Peter Harry was most likely free or freed and the brother of Simeon Harry. Peter Harry was born in Sudbury in 1715.
SA #15105 Original in Sudbury Town Clerk's Office in Church Records	Probably enslaved by Josiah Brown. He was also baptized that day.
Journal of Rev. Israel Loring SA #12192 (transcription)	"Servant maid" indicates that Hannah was enslaved at this time.

Date/Year	Type of Reference (Event)	Name of the Enslaved	Name of Slaveowner (if applicable)
18 Oct. 1742, 10 Oct. 1743	Payment for medical care and for last sickness	Frank	N/A
3 Feb. 1743	Accident	Simeon (Sim)	Rev. Israel Loring
23 Jun. 1743	Runaway slave ad	Sampson, aged 23	Josiah Brown
1745 (after 24 Apr. 1745)	Probate	Nero Benson	Rev. John Swift of Framingham Dr. Ebenezer Roby
11 Oct. 1745	Death	Peter Harry	Unknown
2 Nov. 1745	Bill of sale for slave	Frank (Francis) Benson	Rev. John Swift, Acton Josiah Richardson Sr.
9 Nov. 1746	Church members on the west side.	Nero Benson	Samuel Wood
5 Aug. 1746	Death	Zilpah, "my father's Negro woman died"	Benjamin Wight

Source	Notes
SA #1572, #1580 (transcription); original at Sudbury Town Clerk's Office. Town Records Both entries are in Book III.	Sudbury Town Meeting voted to compensate Dr. Ebenezer Roby for medical care for Frank and Isaac Read for her last sickness (most likely once enslaved by the Read family and freed in Arabella Read's will).
Journal of Rev. Israel Loring SA #12193 (transcription)	"Sim Narrowly escaped of having both his Legs broken by a Log falling upon a Stone before the Schoolhouse Door. A Mercy Which I could take a due notice of and Return God thanks for."
Bly, *Escaping Bondage*, 74, from *Boston Weekly News-Letter*	Possibly the same Samson [Sampson] as 9 Aug. 1741.
Middlesex County, MA: Probate File Papers, 1648–1871. Middlesex Cases 22000–23999, p. 22049.1 Accessed on americanancestrors.org	Rev. Swift left five enslaved persons at his death and broke up the married couple Nero and Dido Dingo Benson. Dido remained in Framingham with Rev. Swift's widow while Nero was bequeathed to Rev. Swift's son-in-law, Dr. Ebenezer Roby of Sudbury. Will dated 1743.
Sudbury Vital Records	Most likely free or freed, but status unknown. Also likely to be the brother of Simeon Harry and son of Frances and Henry Harry. Born 1716.
Goodnow Library Sudbury, Local History Collection Thomas Stearns Papers	Rev. John Swift of Acton inherited Frank from his father, the minister of Framingham, and soon sold him to Josiah Richardson Sr. of Sudbury. According to an email from Denise Dennis, a direct descendant, on Feb. 4, 2023, Frank Benson and Nero were father and son.
SA #15101 Original in Sudbury Town Clerk's Office, Church Records	Nero Benson became a member of the West Side Church.
"Diary of Experience Wight Richardson" Copy of original transcription from the Massachusetts Historical Society at Wayland Museum and Historical Society.	Benjamin Wight was Richardson's father.

Date/Year	Type of Reference (Event)	Name of the Enslaved	Name of Slaveowner (if applicable)
23 Sept. 1747	Surety Bond of Samuel Wood and Declaration of Emancipation from Slavery	Nero Benson	Samuel Wood
1749	Tax list for Sudbury	17 enslaved persons	N/A
1749	Medical care	Cesar	Capt. David Baldwin
19 Mar. 1749	Persons Who Accepted the Church Covenant 1723–1816 (west side)	Francis, Negro servant William, Negro servant	Josiah Richardson (Francis) Samuel Wood (William)
15 Jun. 1749	Accident	Negro Girl	Unknown
5 Jul. 1752; 16 Apr. 1757	Medical care	Negro man	Nathaniel Hasey (presumed owner)
May 1753	West Side Church dispute	Nero Benson	N/A
1754	Slave census	Nine males and five females	No owners listed
1754	Death	Elizabeth Negro	Joseph Noyes

Source	Notes
SA #1668 (transcription only) Original in Sudbury Town Clerk's files, Town Records, Book III	Bond of £100 "to hold harmless" the Town of Sudbury for maintenance of Nero Benson" after he was given his freedom.
Sudbury Town Clerk vault	Puts number of enslaved persons at 17. Names of enslaved and owners not given.
"Account Book of Ebenezer Roby 1749–1764" p. 104 (inclusive) B MS b 121 Boston Medical Lib., Francis A. Countway Lib. of Medicine, Harvard, p. 33	
SA #15105 Original in Sudbury Town Clerk's Office, Church Records.	Francis is almost certainly Francis (aka Frank) Benson. Note that Samuel Wood still remained a slaveowner after emancipating Nero Benson.
Journal of Rev. Israel Loring Scan of original at Goodnow Library, Sudbury SA #12195.	Notes a bad accident at his son Jonathan's house in Marlborough in which a "negro" girl was burned by gunpowder.
"Account Book of Ebenezer Roby 1749–1764" p. 104 (inclusive) B MS b 121 Boston Medical Lib., Francis A. Countway Lib. of Medicine, Harvard	Both visits were for bleeding.
SA #12196 *Journal of Israel Loring*, scan of original in Goodnow Library	Nero Benson admitted that he had "wronged Cornelius Wood in reporting he [Wood] had taken a false oath." Rev. Loring thanked God for settling "the unhappy differences...which endangered still wider breaches in the Church."
Province of Masachusetts Bay slave census, accessed on primaryresearch.org	Ordered by Gov. William Shirley, the slave census required Massachusetts towns to enumerate all slaves over the age of 16.
Sudbury Vital Records	See 1674–75 entry for a similarity of names.

Date/Year	Type of Reference (Event)	Name of the Enslaved	Name of Slaveowner (if applicable)
1754/55	Medical care	Simeon Harry, Negro	N/A
10 Mar./10 May 1755	Sickness and death	Simeon	Rev. Israel Loring
17 May 1755	Death of Susanna Harry	N/A	Unknown status of Susanna
1756	Medical care	Nero Benson	Freed by Samuel Wood in 1747
3 Jul. 1757	Death	Nero Benson	Freed by Samuel Wood in 1747
6 Oct. 1757	Town Meeting Warrant	Most likely Dido (aka Dido Dingo, aka Dido Benson)	Presumably now freed; known to have been enslaved in Framingham
25 Oct. 1757	Town Meeting	Presumably Dido Dingo Benson	Presumed freed

Source	Notes
"Account Book of Ebenezer Roby 17491764," p. 104 (inclusive) B MS b 121 Boston Medical Lib., Francis A. Countway Lib. of Medicine, Harvard	Medical care for Simeon Harry, his wife and sister Susannah Harry. Account settled Oct. 6, 1757. Simeon Harry was born in Sudbury in 1714. Later moved to Framingham but remained in Rev. Loring's West Side Church.
Journal of Rev. Israel Loring SA #12197 Original at Goodnow Library	Covers Simeon's last sickness and death. Simeon died at 21 in Loring Parsonage. He had been given his freedom when he turned 21 and died shortly afterward.
Journal of Rev. Israel Loring SA #12197 Original at Goodnow Library	First and only mention that Hannah, Rev. Loring's freed servant, is Simeon's mother. Also death of Susanna Harry, Hannah's sister. "Died Susanna Harry sister to our hired woman servant Hannah.…The loss of her son and now her sister."
"Account Book of Ebenezer Roby 1749–1764," p. 104 (inclusive) B MS b 121 Boston Medical Lib., Francis A. Countway Lib. of Medicine, Harvard	Account for Nero Benson was paid partially by the Town of Sudbury. The town paid for visits to Nero at the "West Schoolhouse" and the "West Meeting-house."
Journal of Rev. Israel Loring SA #12198 Original at Goodnow Library	Nero died at the "West Schoolhouse" on July 3, 1757. No known place of burial.
Sudbury Town Clerk's Office, Town Records, Book VI	First mention of Dido in Town Records. She was newly widowed, wife of Nero Benson. "To see what the Town will do in Respect to Dido, a Negro woman who is now upon charge in this Town." No last name given.
Sudbury Town Clerk's Office, Town Records, Book VI	"The Town by their Vote Ordered the Select Men of Sudbury, to make strict enquiry who brought Dido into Town." No last name given.

Date/Year	Type of Reference (Event)	Name of the Enslaved	Name of Slaveowner (if applicable)
11 Mar. 1758	Death	Toby	Col. Brown, (only mention of a Colonel is Josiah Brown)
23 Oct. 1758	Town Meeting	Unnamed	Capt. Reynolds Seager
1759–60	Medical care	Negro Girl	John Rice (presumed owner)
20 Feb. 1760	Sale	"a Negro"	Maj. Joseph Curtis
21 Jun. 1760	Petition of Richard Heard	Unnamed enslaved man	Richard Heard
Mar. 1761	Persons Who Accepted the Church Covenant	Caesar, Negro Servant	Col. Brown (presumed Josiah as he was the only Colonel)
17 May 1761	Persons Who Accepted the Church Covenant 1723–1816 (west side)	Dina (Dinah)	Josiah Richardson Sr.
26 Jun. 1761	Marriage	Dinah, Cesar (also spelled Casar)	Dinah, enslaved by Josiah Richardson of Sudbury Cesar, enslaved by Mrs. Love Flint, of Lincoln

Source	Notes
Journal of Rev. Israel Loring SA #12198	"Yesterday Toby the negro servant of Col. Brown departed this life."
SA #1706 Sudbury Town Clerk's Office, Town Records, Book VI	"To Thomas Hayden for Capt. Seagers Mans Rates." Most likely enslaved and possibly named Portsmouth.
"Account Book of Ebenezer Roby 1749–1764," p. 104 (inclusive) B MS b 121 Boston Medical Lib., Francis A. Countway Lib. of Medicine, Harvard	Dr. Roby visited this patient three times.
"The Revolutionary Journal of Col. Jeduthan Baldwin, 1775–1778." Archive.org	Joseph Curtis of Sudbury sale to Jeduthan Baldwin of Brookfield, MA
Massachusetts Archives Collection. v. 79—Military, 1760–1761 Petition of Richard Heard	Petition of Richard Heard for reimbursement for going to get his enslaved man who took ill while serving in the military.
SA #15105 Sudbury Town Clerk's Office, Church Records	Caesar was also baptized on March 22, 1761.
SA #15105 Original in Sudbury Town Clerk's Office, Church Records	Dinah was also baptized on that date.
Lincoln Vital Records	Dinah's marriage is not recorded in the Sudbury Vital Records, but both Cesar and Dinah are listed separately in "Lincoln Marriages Negroes, Etc."

Date/Year	Type of Reference (Event)	Name of the Enslaved	Name of Slaveowner (if applicable)
10 Sept. 1761	Marriage	Hannah Harry, Francis Benson	Hannah had been freed by Rev. Israel Loring Francis Benson, enslaved by Josiah Richardson
23 May 1762	Birth	Cesar, son of Dinah and her husband Cesar of Lincoln	Josiah Richardson
27 May 1762	Death	Cesar, Dinah's husband	Mrs. Love Flint
30 May 1762	Baptism	Cesar, Dinah's son	Josiah Richardson
Aug. 1762	Warning out (town denies residency)	Dido Dingo Benson	N/A
14 Oct. 1762	Marriage	Cuff, Hagar	Col. John Noyes
16 Jan. 1763	Membership in West Side Church	Caesar, Negro servant	Mrs. Brown
1763	Sudbury Census/ Tax Valuation	11 Servants for Life	

Source	Notes
Sudbury Vital Records	It is likely that Hannah is the same person who was enslaved by Rev. Loring, as her sister was referred to as Susanna Harry. Listed separately as: Benson, Francis and Harry, Hannah. No race specified.
"Diary of Experience Wight Richardson"/MHS unpublished manuscript, copy at Wayland Historical Society	Dinah was enslaved by Josiah Richardson of Sudbury, and Cesar was enslaved by Mrs. Love Flint of Lincoln. Young Cesar would belong to his mother's owner.
"Diary of Experience Wight Richardson"/MHS unpublished manuscript, copy at Wayland Historical Society	Death not listed in *Lincoln Vital Records*.
"Israel Loring's Book of Church Records," "Baptisms," copy at the Wayland Historical Society	
"Worcester County, Mass. Warnings 1737–1788" (available on Google Books)	At some point, Dido left Sudbury and was warned out of Shrewsbury with her son William. She returned to Sudbury and was cared for by the town in 1763 and 1764.
Sudbury Vital Records	Listed under Sudbury Marriages Negroes, etc. Both belonged to Col. Noyes.
SA #15101 Original at Sudbury Town Clerk's Office, Church Records	This is presumably the same Caesar who had accepted the Church Covenant in March 1761, as noted above. In 1763, Mrs. Beulah Brown married Rev. Timothy Minott of Concord and moved there. No record as to whether Caesar went with her.
familysearch.org Accessed through MA Archives Collections, valuations of towns in Middlesex County vol. 130.	

Date/Year	Type of Reference (Event)	Name of the Enslaved	Name of Slaveowner (if applicable)
21 Apr. 1763	Poor Assistance Records	Dido Benson	N/A
1764	Sale of slave	Phebey	Josiah Richardson Jr. of Sudbury to Widow Balch of Framingham
26 Feb. 1764	Marriage	Jane Nimery	Likely free
1764	Purchase of coffin	"negro boy"	John Noyes, purchaser of coffin
29 Oct. 1764	Town Meeting	His Negro	Peter Bent
29 Oct. 1764	Town Meeting	Dido Benson	N/A
1765	Lost census of 1765 Sudbury	Lists 15 Negro males and 12 Negro women	N/A
1766	Will	Juba, Candace, Violet, Nancy, Cloe, Nell	David Baldwin
27 Feb. 1767	Birth	Sippio Paul, son of Boston and Annah	Most likely enslaved to Dr. Ebenezer Roby, as his father was still enslaved

Source	Notes
Overseers of the Poor Meeting SA #73 Original at Sudbury Town Clerk's Office, Misc. Records, Bound.	Jabez Puffer for boarding £9.12.8. Samuel Puffer Jr. for shoes £0.5.4.
Courtesy of Framingham History Center Collection, 2002.1072.	Phebey was two years old.
Lynn Vital Records Accessed on archive.org	Jane Nimery of Sudbury married Nicodemus Gigger (Giger) in Lynn, MA. Listed as "Negroes" under marriage.
"Coffins in Ebenezer Staples Account book 1762–1791." Wayland Historical Society	Identity of the boy is uncertain; probably the boy was enslaved and may have belonged to Col. John Noyes.
SA #1751 Original in Town Clerk's Office, Town Records, Book VI.	Town pays Peter Bent for one day's use of his "negro."
SA #1751	Ens. Jabez Puffer is reimbursed for a bed for Dido Benson.
Early Census Making in Massachusetts, 1643–1765: With a Reproduction of the Lost Census of 1765 (recently found) and documents relating thereto. Available on archive.org	Does not designate African Americans as enslaved, freed or free, but the assumption by the census takers was that most would be enslaved. This number is very high in respect to preceding and succeeding years, which gives the number as 11 to 14.
MA Archives, Middlesex County Probate Records #809	All divided among his children. None stayed together regardless of what their relationship might have been. Baldwin died in 1770.
Records of the East Precinct Church, Sudbury 1722–1782 WPA transcription, Wayland Museum & Hist. Soc. files.	Boston, the father, was enslaved by Dr. Ebenezer Roby, unknown status of child as Annah's status is unknown. By 1790, Boston and family are living in Boston and go by the name of Roby. (1790 federal census accessed through familysearch.org.)

Date/Year	Type of Reference (Event)	Name of the Enslaved	Name of Slaveowner (if applicable)
1767	Sale of Slave	Cato	To Jonas Noyes from his father, John Noyes
1767	Probate	Ashbel, Hagar	Daniel Wyman
20 Nov. 1770	Probate	Dinah, Cesar, Francis Benson	Josiah Richardson
1771	Provincial Tax Valuation		12 slaveowners taxed for one slave each
1771	Probate	Negro named Geny	Elizabeth Baldwin
31 Aug. 1772	Probate	Boston (aka Boston Paul and Boston Roby)	Ebenezer Roby Sr. to son, Ebenezer Roby Jr.
11 Nov. 1772	Church membership	Caesar	Servant of Miss Brown
1773	Birth	Venas Paul, daughter of Boston and Annah	Status unknown
8 Apr. 1773	Property Deed for Slave	Portsmouth	Ezekiel Howe

Source	Notes
Original Bill of Sale, Wayland Historical Society	£53 paid.
MA Archives, Middlesex County Probate Records #25848	"freedom clothes"
MA Archives, Middlesex County Court Records, #19023	Dinah and her son Cesar were left to Josiah's wife, Experience, and Francis Benson to his son, Josiah Jr.
Bettye Pruitt Hobbs G.K. Hall, Boston, MA, 1978. Available on a number of websites.	Included those enslaved only between 14 and 45. Only the owners were named: William Baldwin, Peter Bent, Ephraim Curtis, Thomas Damon, Richard Heard, Ezekiel Howe, Jonas Noyes, Nathaiel Reeves, Nathaniel Rice, Josiah Richardson, Ebenezer Roby, Cornelius Wood.
AA: Middlesex County, MA: Probate File Papers, Case No. 817	Left to her "well-beloved friend Cornelius Waldo."
MA Archives, Middlesex County Probate Records #19398	To his daughter Mary, "the use of my Negro man Boston to take care of the garden she shall improve for herself—cut her wood & bringing it to the House & other uses she shall have for him about the house."
SA, Church Membership During the Ministry of Rev. Jacob Bigelow	Listed as a current member, he might be the same Caesar listed in 16 Jan. 1763 entry or possibly a different Caesar, as the person he now served is different. Status uncertain.
Records of the East Precinct Church, Sudbury 1722–1782 WPA transcription, Wayland Museum & Hist. Soc. files.	Boston, the father, was owned by Dr. Ebenener Roby Jr.; unknown status of child. By 1790, Boston and family were living in Boston and went by the name of Roby.
SA #14737 Original in Wayside Inn Archives	Purchase from the estate of Capt. Reynolds Seager, Sudbury. Administered by William Baldwin.

Date/Year	Type of Reference (Event)	Name of the Enslaved	Name of Slaveowner (if applicable)
May 1773	Death	Slave	Capt. Wood (Cornelius)
1 Jan. 1774	Report of Death	Cesar, Dinah's son	Experience Wight Richardson
1 May 1774	Death	Hannah (Harry), wife of Francis Benson	N/A
29 Mar. 1775	Probate Inventory	Cato	Jonas Noyes
1 Apr. 1775	Birth	Cesar Paul, son of Boston and Annah	Unknown
27 Apr. 1775	Enlistment from Sudbury in the Revolutionary War	Jacob Speen (Spean)	N/A

Source	Notes
SA #12294 Burial Records of Rev. Jacob Bigelow's Parishioners, west side Church	
"Experience Richardson Diary 1728-1782," unpublished manuscript at Massachusetts Historical Society; copy at Wayland Museum & Historical Society.	Experience Wight Richardson reported on this date that the death of Cesar, son of Dinah, occurred sometime during 1773.
SA #12294 Burial Records of Rev. Jacob Bigelow's Parishioners 1772-1816. Original in Town Clerk's Office	Presumably Rev. Loring's freed servant, Hannah.
Original in Noyes file, Wayland Historical Society	£53 valued in inventory—same as purchase price in 1767.
Records of the East Precinct Church, Sudbury 1722-1782 WPA transcription, Wayland Museum & Hist. Soc. files.	Boston, the father, was enslaved by Dr. Ebenener Roby Jr. Unknown status of child and of the mother. By 1790, Boston and family are living in Boston and go by the name of Roby.
Massachusetts Soldiers and Sailors in the Revolutionary War Quintal, *Patriots of Color*, 203	Served throughout the Revolutionary War, but only once gave Sudbury as his residence. He fought at Bunker Hill for Sudbury. Known to have lived in Natick at times throughout the war. He was listed as "negro." He might have been of mixed race but was almost certainly part Indian, as the Speen family were original founders of the Praying Indian town of Natick. His height was listed as 5'8" and his birth circa 1754. In 1776, he was listed as living in Cambridge and married Dinah Pero on Feb. 2.

Date/Year	Type of Reference (Event)	Name of the Enslaved	Name of Slaveowner (if applicable)
30 Apr. 1775	Enlistment from Sudbury in the Revolutionary War	Cuff Nimrod (Nimro, Nimroo, Nimroe, later Nims)	N/A
31 May 1775	Enlistment	Porter Cuddy	N/A
7 Oct. 1775	End of service from Sudbury in the Revolutionary War	Nicodemus Gigger (Giger, Gidger)	N/A
9 Dec. 1776	Emancipation	Dinah	Experience Wight Richardson
30 Jan. 1777	Marriage	Frank Benson (formerly enslaved)	N/A
13 Apr. 1777	Enlistment from Sudbury in the Revolutionary War	Fortune Homer	N/A

Source	Notes
Massachusetts Soldiers and Sailors in the Revolutionary War Quintal, *Patriots of Color*, 163	Cuff enlisted for eight months' service and fought at the Battle of Bunker Hill. There is no other record of service for him in the Revolutionary War. He listed his residence as Sudbury. No race was specified, but he appears on several lists of Patriots of Color from Massachusetts. On January 14, 1779, he married Alice Kent in Natick. He was still listed as "of Sudbury."
Patriots of Color, 90 *Metrowest Daily News*, July 24, 2011	He is listed as "negro." He served for 62 days for Sudbury, which was listed as his residence, and enlisted for a short time from Plymouth County in 1776. No further record or information at this time.
"MASSOG Vol. 36, No. 2, 2012," published by the Massachusetts Society of Genealogists, Inc., 43–48. Massachusetts Soldiers . and Sailors in the Revolutionary War, vol. 6, 400	Nicodemus's length of service was not specified, but it ended on Oct. 7, 1775. In 1777, he married his third wife, Beulah (Speen) Rogers, in Natick and was listed as head of household in Natick in the 1790 federal census. He died in Natick on May 19, 1802. His race is uncertain other than he was a person of color—Indian, African American or a combination of both.
"Experience Richardson Diary," 1728–1782, unpublished manuscript at Massachusetts Historical Society; copy at Wayland Museum & Historical Society	"This day my servant Diner [*sic*] had hir [*sic*] freedom."
Concord, MA Vital Records	Marriage of Frank (Francis) Benson and Roseanna Lewis. Francis (Frank) was the widower of Hannah Harry, who died in Sudbury in 1774. See other entries.
Massachusetts Soldiers and Sailors in the Revolutionary War, vol. 8, 209	Served in the Continental army and reported "died on April 20, 1777." No other service was reported prior to 1777.

Date/Year	Type of Reference (Event)	Name of the Enslaved	Name of Slaveowner (if applicable)
16 Sep. 1777	Tax Valuation/Census	6 Negroes	
10 Dec. 1779	Receipt for payment for slave	"Negro girl"	Ezekiel Howe
28 Dec. 1779	Birth	Hannah Harry Benson, daughter of Frank and Rosanna Benson	
2 Dec. 1780	Enlistment in the Revolutionary War from East Sudbury	Samuel Ephraim	N/A
8 Feb. 1781	Marriage	Dinah Young of Sudbury, Cuff Kneeland of Lincoln	Both freed, previously enslaved
11 Mar. 1781	Death	Cuff Kneeland (Dinah's husband)	N/A
14 Jun. 1781	Birth	Boston Paul, son of Boston and Annah	Status unknown

Source	Notes
Microfilm copy found in the Census file at the Wayland Historical Society	
Wayside Inn Archives; Howe Collection, Legal Documents, Folder 7 & 8, 172C SA #14738	As of this writing, last documented purchase of an enslaved person in Sudbury.
Concord, MA Vital Records	I believe that Hannah's mother is the same woman later known as Rose Benson and that Frank named his daughter after his first wife, Hannah Harry, whom he married while enslaved to Josiah Richardson in Sudbury. Frank Benson and Rosanna Lewis were married in Concord in 1777.
Massachusetts Soldiers and Sailors in the Revolutionary War, vol. 5, 385	Samuel Ephraim was a Natick Praying Indian. He was engaged to serve to the credit of East Sudbury (right after the town divided), and it is unlikely that he ever lived in East Sudbury (now Wayland). He was 17 years old and remained in the service until 1782. He is listed on the Forgotten Patriots DAR website as a person of color who enlisted from East Sudbury.
Sudbury Vital Records	Extremely likely this is Dinah, who was previously enslaved to Josiah and, later, Experience Richardson and freed in 1776. Their race was not specified in Lincoln and Sudbury vital records. In Sudbury, Kneeland was misspelled as Reland.
Lincoln Vital Records	
Wayland Vital Records 1790 Federal Census accessed on familysearch.org	Boston, the father, was enslaved by Drs. Ebenener Roby Sr. and Jr., unknown status of child. By 1790, Boston and family were living in Boston and going by the name of Roby.

Date/Year	Type of Reference (Event)	Name of the Enslaved	Name of Slaveowner (if applicable)
22 Jan. 1783	Marriage	Dinah Kneelee (Kneeland)	Dinah freed, Cato Walker freed
29 Oct. 1787	Town Meeting Payment for Work	Francis Benson (not identified by race)	N/A
1796	Codicil to will of Ezekiel Howe, Sudbury	Portsmouth, old Negro servant, presumed freed	
26 Aug. 1799	Death	Portsmouth, a Negro about 70	
25 Mar. 1803	Support of Rose Benson	Rose Benson, (presumed widow of Frank Benson)	

Source	Notes
Sudbury Vital Records	Dinah's last name had various spellings, including Kneelee and Nealen, all corruptions of Kneeland. Cato Walker was from Worcester.
East Sudbury Town Meeting Minutes, Vol. 1, 1780–1817, Wayland Town Clerk's Office	At the same Town Meeting, William Negro was also paid for work. Could this be William Benson? He is reported to have died in Framingham about 1790.
SA #14755 Original in Wayside Inn Archives, Sudbury, MA.	"My old Negro servant Portsmouth shall be subject to the orders of my wife aforesaid in such matters and things as may be necessary in assisting her about her household concerns and such servant shall be well and comfortably supported through life, both in sickness and health…and after his decease be buried in decent and Christian burial." There is no known gravesite for Portsmouth as of this writing.
SA #12294 Burial Records of Rev. Jacob Bigelow's Parishioners 1772–1816. Original in Sudbury Town Clerk's Office, Church Records	
SA # 2493 Town Meeting Warrant, Mar. 25, 1803 Wayland Town Clerk's Office, Town Records, Book VII	"To see if the Town, will take any Measures, for defraying the expence [*sic*] of a demand, made by the Inhabitants of the Town of Concord, against the Town of Sudbury, for the support of Rose Benson; (a Negro Woman) now resideing [*sic*] in said Town of Concord." It is almost certain that Rose and Rosanna are one and the same.

Date/Year	Type of Reference (Event)	Name of the Enslaved	Name of Slaveowner (if applicable)
4 Apr. 1803	Payment to Concord	Rose Benson	
2 Jun. 1803	Death	"a Negro, widow of Frank Benson"	
1824	East Sudbury letter denying Boston's claim for payment	Mary Sinnes	
1904	Family history	Slaves	Col. John Noyes (1715–1785)

Source	Notes
SA #2494 (transcription) Original in Wayland Town Clerk's Office, Town Records, Book VII	"The Town by their Vote directed their Treasurer, to Borrow a sum of Money, sufficient, together with what is Now in the Treasury, that is Unappropriated, to satisfy the demand, made by the inhabitants of the Town of Concord, for the support of Rose Benson, a Negro woman." Apparently the town treasurer paid Concord with his own money, as he was reimbursed by the Town of Sudbury at long last on July 1, 1805, at Town Meeting.
Burial Records of Rev. Jacob Bigelow's Parishioners 1772–1816 Original at Sudbury Town Clerk's Office, Church Records	Presumably this is Rose Benson who returned to Sudbury in the late winter or early spring of 1803. This conclusion came from Poor Records and other scanned documents sent to me by Nathaniel Smith, Town of Concord archivist.
Letter from Overseers of the Poor of the Town of East Sudbury to Overseers of the Poor of Boston. Original at the Wayland Historical Society	Letter concerns Mary Sinnes, resident of Boston and granddaughter of Boston (Paul, later Roby), once enslaved by Dr. Ebenezer Roby. Her mother was Venus Paul, listed in Wayland Vital Records as born in 1773. East Sudbury denied any responsibility for Mary Sinnes's care as her mother (Venus) was never enslaved in East Sudbury. "The parents [Boston and Annah] we doubt not were slaves, at, and after [Venus's] birth." Venus was exempted from servitude retroactively after the Massachusetts Constitution and 1783 freedom suit cases, according to the letter from the East Sudbury Board of Overseers citing the 1819 MA Supreme Judicial Court Ruling in *Inhabitants of Lanesborough v. Inhabitants of Westfield*.
Genealogical Records of Some of the Noyes Descendants of James, Nicholas and Peter, vol 2. Accessed at archives.org	"Col. Noyes owned much real estate and a considerable number of slaves."

NOTES

Chapter 1

1. Background material in this section is largely drawn from Moore, *Notes on the History of Slavery in Massachusetts*; Zilversmit, *First Emancipation*; and Greene, *Negro in Colonial New England*.
2. The original name of Massachusetts from 1630 to 1690. From 1691 to 1774, Massachusetts was a province headed by a governor appointed by the British Crown.
3. Hardesty, *Black Lives, Native Lands, White Worlds*, 92.
4. Berlin, *Many Thousands Gone*, 47.
5. Greene, *Negro in Colonial New England*, 73.
6. founders.archives.gov (National Archives), "From John Adams to Robert J. Evans, 8 June 1819."

Chapter 2

7. See appendix, "Timeline," 9 Jan. 1654.
8. Lydia Maria Child (1802–1880) lived in Wayland from 1853 until her death in 1880. She is buried in North Cemetery in Wayland.
9. Thompson, *Sex in Middlesex*, 159.
10. SA #468. Original in Sudbury Town Clerk's Office, Town Records Book I.

11. Noyes and Noyes, *Genealogical Record of Some of the Noyes Descendants*, 52.
12. Ibid., 45.
13. Hudson, *History of Sudbury*, 451–52.
14. Ibid., 606.
15. Wall, *Reminiscences of Worcester from the Earliest Period*, 50.
16. Forbes, *Hundredth Town*, 169.
17. See, Appendix A: Timeline 1705/08.
18. Wall, *Reminiscences of Worcester from the Earliest Period*, 56–57.
19. See appendix, "Timeline," 1701.
20. See appendix, "Timeline," 1717.
21. See appendix, "Timeline," 18 Oct. 1742, 10 Oct. 1743.
22. Gragg, *Quest for Security*, ch. 9.

Chapter 3

23. Background material on homelife comes primarily from Greene and Hardesty. Loring quotes are from his *Journal*.
24. Greene, *Negro in Colonial New England*, 101.
25. Hardesty, *Black Lives, Native Lands, White Worlds*, 92.
26. Variant spelling of Howe is How. I have used the one with the added *e*, except for Jerusha, who preferred How. Dates on Ezekiel's proprietorship varied from 1744 to 1749.
27. How, "Journal of Jerusha How," 22.
28. Garfield and Ridley, *As Ancient Is This Hostelry*, 78–79.
29. See appendix, "Timeline," 1796.
30. Hardesty, *Black Lives, Native Lands, White Worlds*, 52.
31. Bly, *Escaping Bondage*, 74.
32. Hudson, *History of Sudbury*, 325. The spelling of Brown sometimes included an *e* on the end.

Chapter 4

33. Greene, *Negro in Colonial New England*, ch. 8, 191–217.
34. See appendix, "Timeline," 1764, sale of slave.
35. "Experience Wight Richardson (1728–1782) Diary."
36. See appendix, "Timeline," 1745, probate of Reverend John Swift of Framingham.

Chapter 5

37. Background material based on information from Professor Richard J. Boles, including email exchanges in December 2023, his book *Dividing the Faith*, the November 30, 2023 program sponsored by the Partnership of Historic Bostons and book talk April 3, 2021, Maine Historical Societey.
38. Author's notes and email exchange following his program of the night before, February 17, 2023. Dr. Minkema is executive director of the Jonathan Edwards Center, Yale Divinity School.
39. Boles, *Dividing the Faith*, 30–31.
40. Ibid., 20.
41. Ibid., 27.
42. Loring, *Journal*, 15 Nov. 1736 and 9 Dec. 1736.
43. Higginbotham, *In the Matter of Color*, 75.
44. See appendix, "Timeline," 9 Nov. 1746.
45. Loring, *Journal*, 25 Apr. and 13 May 1753.

Chapter 6

46. See appendix, "Timeline," Aug 1762.
47. See appendix, "Timeline," 21 Apr. 1763.
48. See appendix, "Timeline," 29 Oct. 1764.
49. See appendix, "Timeline," 2 Nov. 1745.
50. See appendix, "Timeline," 19 Mar. 1749.
51. See appendix, "Timeline," 10 Sept. 1761.
52. See appendix, "Timeline," 20 Nov. 1770.
53. See appendix, "Timeline," 1 May 1774.
54. Gross, *Minutemen and Their World*, 116.
55. Emerson, *Diaries and Letters of William Emerson*, 20.
56. 1780 Concord Tax List, scan sent via email by Nathaniel Smith, archivist for the Town of Concord, Massachusetts.
57. Assessor's Records, Town Tax 13 June 1783, Report of Philomen Brown, Collector for East Sudbury. Prior to the town's formal separation, assessments stipulated whether the person resided on the east or west side.
58. See appendix, "Timeline," 29 Oct. 1787.
59. Information on Rose Benson was provided by Concord town archivist Nathaniel Smith in personal correspondence of scanned documents, including poor records, of the town of Concord, Massachusetts.

60. See appendix, "Timeline," 23 Mar. 1803 and 4 Apr. 1803.
61. See appendix, "Timeline," 2 Jun. 1803.

Chapter 7

62. Background material includes Greene, *Negro in Colonial New England*, ch. 5, 124–43.
63. Hardesty, *Black Lives, Native Lands, White Worlds*, 64.
64. Murray Philomen was deeded approximately twelve acres by his owner, Benjamin Harrington, in 1756. Information courtesy of Weston Historical Society.
65. See appendix, "Timeline," 1771 Provincial Tax Valuation.
66. See appendix, "Timeline," 1754 slave census.
67. See appendix, "Timeline," 1763 Sudbury Census/Tax Valuation.
68. See appendix, "Timeline," Lost Census of 1765.
69. Benton, *Early Census Making in Massachusetts*, 55.
70. Massachusetts included Maine until it became a state in 1820.
71. americanancestors.org and familysearch.org both provide free access.
72. See appendix, "Timeline," 1766.
73. See appendix, "Timeline," 29 Mar. 1775.
74. See appendix, "Timeline," 20 Nov. 1770.
75. See appendix, "Timeline," 1767 probate.
76. A full list of vital records used is in the bibliography.
77. See bibliography.

Chapter 8

78. Robinson, "Sudbury and Wayland Muster for the Revolution of 1775."

Chapter 9

79. Quintal, *Patriots of Color*, 17.
80. Cuff is listed as Nims in Sudbury Vital Records and Nimro in Natick Vital Records.
81. At the time of his marriage, Jacob Speen is listed as "of Cambridge."
82. See appendix, "Timeline," 7 Oct. 1775.

83. Massachusetts Office of the Secretary of State, *Massachusetts Soldiers and Sailors in the Revolutionary War*, 5: 385.
84. Hardesty, *Black Lives, Native Lands, White Worlds*, 102.

Chapter 10

85. Ibid., 119.
86. Powell, *Puritan Villlage*, 93.
87. For a more detailed account see John Hannigan, "Enslavement and Enlistment," on the National Park Service website.
88. See appendix, "Timeline," 22 Jan. 1783.

Chapter 11

89. Background material from Zilversmit, *First Emancipation*, 112–17.
90. See appendix, "Timeline," 10 Dec. 1779.
91. See appendix, "Timeline," 1824.

Chapter 12

92. Greene, *Negro in Colonial New England*, 299.
93. Rabushka, *Taxation in Colonial America*, 169.
94. Valuation lists for the town of Wayland, Massachusetts, originals at Wayland Town Building, Board of Assessors.

Conclusion

95. Hardesty, *Black Lives, Native Lands, White Worlds*, 119.
96. The reference is to Nero Benson, Frank Benson's father, who was a member of the West Side Church.
97. Thomas Stearns Collection, Goodnow Library, Sudbury, Massachusetts, Local History Collection.

BIBLIOGRAPHY

Books and Ebooks

Adams, Catherine, and Elizabeth H. Pleck. *Love of Freedom: Black Women in Colonial and Revolutionary New England.* Oxford: Oxford University Press, 2010.

Baker, Emerson W. *A Storm of Witchcraft.* Oxford: Oxford University Press, 2015.

Barry, William. *A History of Framingham, Massachusetts, Including the Plantation, from 1640 to the Present Time.* Boston: James Munroe and Company, 1847. (Ebook archive.org)

Benton, Josiah Henry, Jr. *Early Census Making in Massachusetts 1643–1765, with a Reproduction of the Lost Census of 1765 (Recently Found).* Boston: Charles E. Goodspeed, 1905.

———. *Warning Out in New England 1656–1817.* Boston: W.B. Clarke Company, 1911. (Ebook archive.org)

Berlin, Ira. *Many Thousands Gone: The First Two Centuries of Slavery in North America.* Cambridge, MA: Belknap Press of Harvard University Press, 1998.

Blake, Francis E. *Worcester County, Massachusetts, Warnings, 1737–1788.* Worcester, MA: Franklin P. Rice, 1899. (On archive.org)

Bly, Antonio T., ed. *Escaping Bondage.* Lanham, MD: Lexington Books, 2012.

Boles, Richard J. *Dividing the Faith: The Rise of Segregated Churches in the Early American North.* New York: New York University Press, 2020.

Child, Lydia Maria. *An Appeal in Favor of That Class of Americans Called Africans.* Amherst: University of Massachusetts, 1996.

Daughters of the American Revolution. Forgotten Patriots: African American and American Indian Patriots in the Revolutionary War (database). 2011. www.dar.org/library/research-guides/forgotten-patriots.

Dayton, Cornelia H., and Sharon V. Sallinger. *Robert Love's Warnings.* Philadelphia: University of Pennsylvania Press, 2014.

Emery, Helen Fitch. *The Puritan Village Evolves.* Canaan, NH: Phoenix Publishing, 1981.

Fischer, David Hackett. *Paul Revere's Ride.* New York: Oxford University Press, 1994.

Foner, Eric. *Tom Paine and Revolutionary America.* London: Oxford University Press, 1976.

Forbes, Harriette Merrifield. *The Hundredth Town: Glimpses of Life in Westborough 1717–1817.* Boston: Press of Rockwell and Churchill, 1889. (archive.org)

Garfield, Curtis F., and Alison R. Ridley. *As Ancient Is This Hostelry: The Story of The Wayside Inn.* Sudbury, MA: Porcupine Press, 1988.

Gragg, Larry. *A Quest for Security: The Life of Samuel Parris 1653–1720.* Westport, CT: Praeger, 1990.

Greene, Lorenzo J. *The Negro in Colonial New England 1620–1776.* Eastford, CT: Martino Fine Books, 2017. (Ebook archive.org)

Gross, Robert A. *The Minutemen and Their World (Revised and Expanded Edition).* New York: Picador, 2022.

Hardesty, Jared Ross. *Black Lives, Native Lands, White Worlds: A History of Slavery in New England.* Amherst: University of Massachusetts Press, 2019.

Higginbotham, A. Leon, Jr. *In the Matter of Color: Race and the American Legal System: The Colonial Period:* New York: Oxford University Press, 1978.

Hudson, Alfred Sereno. *The History of Sudbury, Massachusetts.* Sudbury, MA: Sudbury Press, 1968. Reprint of 1889 book. (Ebook archive.org)

Lincoln, William. *History of Worcester, Massachusetts: From Its Earliest Settlement to September 1836; with Various Notices Relating to the History of Worcester County.* United Kingdom: M.D. Phillips, 1837. (Ebook archive.org)

Massachusetts Office of the Secretary of State. *Massachusetts Soldiers and Sailors of the Revolutionary War.* 17 vols. Boston: Wright and Potter Print Co., State Printers, 1896–1908. (various online sites)

McManus, Edgar J. *Black Bondage in the North.* Syracuse, NY: Syracuse University Press, 1973.

Melish, Joanne Pope. *Disowning Slavery.* Ithaca, NY: Cornell University Press, 1998.

Moore, George. *Notes on the History of Slavery in Massachusetts*. New York: Negro Universities Press, 1968. (Google books)

O'Brien, Jean M. *Dispossession by Degrees: Indian Land and Identity in Natick, Massachusetts, 1650–1790*. Lincoln: University of Nebraska Press, 2003.

Powell, Sumner Chilton. *Puritan Village*. Hanover, NH: Wesleyan University Press, 1963.

Quintal, George, Jr. *Patriots of Color: 'A Peculiar Beauty and Merit.'* Boston: National Park Service: Boston National Historical Park, 2004. (Online Boston National Historical Park)

Rabushka, Alvin. *Taxation in Colonial America*. Princeton, NJ: Princeton University Press, 2008.

Romer, Robert H. *Slavery in the Connecticut Valley of Massachusetts*. Florence, MA: Levellers Press, 2009.

Sewall, Samuel. "The Selling of Joseph: A Memorial." Lincoln: University of Nebraska (electronic copy of 1700 publication on archive.org.)

Temple, Josiah H. *History of Framingham, Massachusetts 1640–1885*. Framingham, MA: New England History Press, 1988. Repr. of 1887 edition. (Ebook archives.org)

Thompson, Roger. *Sex in Middlesex*. Amherst: University of Massachusetts Press, 1986.

Wall, Caleb Arnold. *Reminiscences of Worcester from the Earliest Period*. Worcester, MA: Tyler & Seagrave, 1877. (Online archive.org)

Wall, Patricia Q. *Lives of Consequence: Blacks in Early Kittery & Berwick in the Massachusetts Province of Maine*. Portsmouth, NH: Portsmouth Historical Society, 2017.

Wiggin, Richard C. *Embattled Farmers*. Lincoln, MA: Lincoln Historical Society, 2013.

Zilversmit, Arthur. *The First Emancipation: The Abolition of Slavery in the North*. Chicago: University of Chicago Press, 1967.

Family Histories and Town Records

Baldwin, Thomas W. *Vital Records of Framingham, Massachusetts to the Year 1850*. Boston: Wright & Potter, 1911.

———. *Vital Records of Natick, Massachusetts to the Year 1850*. Boston: Stanhope Press, 1910.

Benson, Richard H. *The Benson Family of Colonial Massachusetts*. Boston: Newbury Street Press, 2003. (Digitized by Boston Public Library; ebook archive.org)

Essex Institute. *Vital Records of Lynn, Massachusetts, to the Year 1849.* Salem, MA, 1905. (archive.org)

New England Historic Genealogical Society. *Vital Records of Lincoln, Massachusetts to the Year 1850.* Boston, 1908. (archive.org)

———. *Vital Records of Sudbury, Massachusetts, to the Year 1850.* Boston, 1903. (archive.org)

———. *Vital Records of Wayland, Massachusetts to the Year 1850.* Boston, 1910. (archive.org)

Noyes, Col. Henry E., and Harriette E. Noyes. *Genealogical Record of Some of the Noyes Descendants.* Vol. 2. Boston, 1904. (ebook archive.org)

Sokolow, Michael. *Charles Benson, Mariner of Color in the Age of Sail.* Amherst: University of Massachusetts Press, 2003.

Tolman, George. *Concord, Massachusetts Births, Marriages, and Deaths, 1635–1850.* Boston: T. Todd, 1895.

Town of Wayland Board of Assessors. "Valuation Lists for the Town of Wayland 1780–1820." Originals at Wayland Town Building.

Wall, Caleb A. *Reminiscences of Worcester from the Earliest Period.* Worcester, MA: Printed by Tyler and Seagrave, 1877.

Diaries and Journals

Baldwin, Jeduthan. "The Revolutionary Journal of Col. Jeduthan Baldwin, 1775–1778." Bangor, ME, 1906. (Page images on HathiTrust)

Emerson, Amelia Forbes, ed. *The Diaries and Letters of William Emerson 1743–1776.* Private printing, 1972.

How, Jerusha. "Journal of Jerusha How." Original at Goodnow Library, Sudbury, MA, 1838–1841. (on Sudbury Archives #12208)

Loring, Reverend Israel. *Journal of Rev. Israel Loring.* Scans of the originals and number of transcriptions of originals are at the Local History Center at Goodnow Library in Sudbury, MA. Locations of the transcribed originals are currently unknown. Entries cover the years 1704–1765 with some gaps and can be found on the Sudbury Archives website.

Richardson, Experience Wight. "Experience Wight Richardson (1728–1782) Diary." Massachusetts Historical Society unpublished transcription, copy at Wayland Museum and Historical Society.

Roby, Dr. Ebenezer. *Account Book of Ebenezer Roby, 1749–1764* (inclusive). B MS b121. Boston Medical Library, Francis A. Countway Library of Medicine, Harvard University, Boston, 1937–1938. (on internet archive)

————. "Accounts of Dr. Ebenezer Roby, Showing Names of Patients and Charges for Medicines and Attendance, March 25, 1730–May 17, 1731." Transcribed by the Works Progress Administration as part of Middlesex County Historical Survey.

Winthrop, Governor John. *The Journal of John Winthrop 1630–1649.* Original at Massachusetts Historical Society, Boston. (on archive.org)

Church Records

Bigelow, Jacob. "Burial Records of Rev. Jacob Bigelow's Parishioners." Sudbury Town Clerk's Office, Church Records and Vital Records, bound volume handwritten; scanned and transcribed on Sudbury Archives #12294.

————. "Church Records During Ministry of Rev. Jacob Bigelow 1772–1813." Sudbury Town Clerk's Office, Church Records; microfilm; scanned and transcribed on Sudbury Archives #12291.

Loring, Israel. "Book of Church Records Maintained by Him as Pastor of the Church in Sudbury and of the Westside Church until His Death in March 1772 and Maintained by Other Hands Thereafter." Copied Feb. 1979 from microfilm of the original, which is in the possession of the Unitarian Church in Sudbury, MA; 2 scanned copies in the files of the Wayland Historical Society.

————. "List of Persons Who Accepted the Church Covenant March 31, 1723–September 29, 1816." Sudbury Town Clerk's Office, Church Records, bound volume, handwritten; Sudbury Archives #15105.

————. "List of West Parish Church Members." Sudbury Town Clerk's Office, Church Records, bound volume, handwritten; scanned and transcribed on Sudbury Archives #15101.

Works Progress Administration. *Records of the East Precinct Church Sudbury, Massachusetts 1722–1782.* Middlesex County Historical Survey, 1937–38. Transcription of original records of First Parish Unitarian Church, Wayland, MA; 2 copies at Wayland Museum and Historical Society.

Articles, Online and Printed

Bell, J.L. "I do therefore…free him and discharge him." *Boston 1775* blogspot, February 19, 2009.

Desrochers, Robert E., Jr. "Slave-for-Sale Advertisements and Slavery in Massachusetts, 1704–1781." *William and Mary Quarterly* 59, no. 3 (July 2002). (jstor.org)

Dutton, Thomas L. "The People Who Had Vanished." *Unseen Neighbors: Native Americans of Central Massachusetts*, 1997. (wordpress.com)

Hannigan, John. "Enslavement and Enlistment." NPS (National Park Service website), 2014.

Mackinlay, Peter W. "The New England Puritan Attitude Toward Black Slavery." *Old Time New England* 63, no. 231 (Winter 1973). (amazon.aws)

Robinson, Barbara. "Sudbury and Wayland Muster for the Revolution of 1775." Reprinted from the *Town Crier* Bicentennial Supplement, June 19, 1975.

Twombly, Robert C., and Robert H. Moore. "Black Puritan: The Negro in Seventeenth-Century Massachusetts." *William and Mary Quarterly* 24, no. 3 (April 1967). (jstor)

Chief Primary Online and Print Sources

Online resources are not a substitute for original documents, but they can be extremely useful, especially when it is difficult to visit repositories in person, as during the recent COVID pandemic. If there is any doubt that the information might not be correct, as when only the transcriptions are online, it is imperative to go to the source. Primary source documents were accessed both in person and on websites. Several websites deserve special mention because of their relevance and frequency of use.

The Church of Jesus Christ of Latter-day Saints. Family Search (database). familysearch.org.

Comparable to Ancestry.com but free of charge, Family Search is an indispensable aid to genealogical research including vital records, census, probate, court and military records.

Goodnow Library. Sudbury Archives (database). archives.sudbury. ma.us/Presto/home/home.aspx.

A searchable database of historic records relating to Sudbury, Middlesex County, Massachusetts, 1639–1850, compiled from Town of Sudbury records. Includes, but is not limited to, Town Meetings, warrants, personal papers, diaries and journals, poor assistance records and church records. It includes archives from the town clerk's office, Goodnow Library, Wayside Inn and the Wayland Historical Society. Please note that Wayland records are only covered up to 1780, when the town divided. This is a first stop for all subsequent research.

Internet Archive (database). archive.org.

Internet Archive provided online access to a number of books no longer under copyright.

Massachusetts State Archives

Indispensible resource online and in person of records relating to the history of Massachusetts, including military records, probate, court and vital records. Special mention to Caitlin Jones, who sent me all the information I sought during the COVID pandemic when I could no longer go in person. Many records in the State Archives can be accessed on Family Search.

New England Historic Genealogic Society. American Ancestors (database). www.americanancestors.org.

Especially helpful were searchable databases of Middlesex County, MA probate records and Middlesex County, MA court records. Probate records were available free of charge, and court records required a small fee. All records were scans of the original documents.

Many probate and court records are also available on Family Search and Ancestry.com.

INDEX

The author viewing Nero Benson's emancipation documents taken at the town clerk's office, Sudbury. *Photo by Francesco Buccella, archivist, Sudbury Historical Society.*

ABOUT THE AUTHOR

J ane Sciacca is a retired ranger in the National Park Service with a degree in history education from Simmons University. Jane has studied New England slavery and abolition for many years. Her work as an interpreter for the National Park Service in Concord, Boston and Cambridge led to her interest in researching enslavement and abolition in her own community of Wayland, where she has lived with her family for over fifty years. Jane has written a children's book, *Mr. Francis Saves the City*, for Lowell National Historical Park, where it has been sold for over twenty years. She has authored several articles for *Cobblestone Magazine* on the start of the American Revolution in Lexington and Concord, as well as guidebooks for Minute Man National Historical Park. She has researched and presented numerous programs, both online and in person, including on John Brown of Harpers Ferry fame and Wayland's own Lydia Maria Child, author and human rights advocate committed to the abolition of slavery and the elimination of discrimination against people of color in the nineteenth century. Jane has been an active member of the Wayland Historical Society for many years, serving as president and curator. As chair of the Wayland Historical Commission, a Wayland town board, she oversaw the 1981 publication of the first history of Wayland as a separate town, *The Puritan Village Evolves*. Her overriding passion lies in telling stories of persons overlooked in history books, including the enslaved, nineteenth-century abolitionists and women.

Visit us at
www.historypress.com